THE SALVAGING OF CIVILIZATION

THE PROBABLE FUTURE OF MANKIND

THE SALVAGING OF CIVILIZATION

THE PROBABLE FUTURE OF MANKIND

BY

H. G. WELLS

New York
THE MACMILLAN COMPANY
1921

THE SALVAGING OF CIVILIZATION
THE PROBABLE FUTURE OF MANKIND

THE SALVAGING OF CIVILIZATION

I

THE PROBABLE FUTURE OF MANKIND[*]

§ 1

THE present outlook of human affairs is one that admits of broad generalizations and that seems to require broad generalizations. We are in one of those phases of experience which become cardinal in history. A series of immense and tragic events have shattered the self-complacency and challenged the will and intelligence of mankind. That easy general forward movement of human affairs which for several generations had seemed to justify the persuasion of a necessary and invincible progress, progress towards greater powers, greater happiness, and a continual enlargement of life, has been checked violently and perhaps arrested altogether. The spectacular catastrophe of the great war has revealed an accumulation of destructive forces in our outwardly prosperous society, of which few of us had dreamt; and it has

* First published in the *Review of Reviews*.

1

also revealed a profound incapacity to deal with and restrain these forces. The two years of want, confusion, and indecision that have followed the great war in Europe and Asia, and the uncertainties that have disturbed life even in the comparatively untouched American world, seem to many watchful minds even more ominous to our social order than the war itself. What is happening to our race? they ask. Did the prosperities and confident hopes with which the twentieth century opened, mark nothing more than a culmination of fortuitous good luck? Has the cycle of prosperity and progress closed? To what will this staggering and blundering, the hatreds and mischievous adventures of the present time, bring us? Is the world in the opening of long centuries of confusion and disaster such as ended the Western Roman Empire in Europe or the Han prosperity in China? And if so, will the débâcle extend to America? Or is the American (and Pacific?) system still sufficiently removed and still sufficiently autonomous to maintain a progressive movement of its own if the Old World collapse?

Some sort of answer to these questions, vast and vague though they are, we must each one of us have before we can take an intelligent interest or cast an effective vote in foreign affairs. Even though a man formulate no definite answer, he must still have an implicit persuasion before he can act in these matters. If he have no clear conclusions openly arrived at, then he must act upon subconscious conclusions instinctively arrived at. Far better is it that he should bring them into the open light of thought.

The suppression of war is generally regarded as central to the complex of contemporary problems. But war is not a new thing in human experience, and for scores of centuries mankind has managed to get along in spite of its frequent recurrence. Most states and empires have been intermittently at war throughout their periods of stability and prosperity. But their warfare was not the warfare of the present time. The thing that has brought the rush of progressive development of the past century and a half to a sudden shock of arrest is not the old and familiar warfare, but warfare strangely changed and exaggerated by novel conditions. It is this change in conditions, therefore, and not war itself, which is the reality we have to analyze in its bearing upon our social and political ideas. In 1914 the European Great Powers resorted to war, as they had resorted to war on many previous occasions, to decide certain open issues. This war flamed out with an unexpected rapidity until all the world was involved; and it developed a horror, a monstrosity of destructiveness, and, above all, an inconclusiveness quite unlike any preceding war. That unlikeness was the essence of the matter. Whatever justifications could be found for its use in the past, it became clear to many minds that under the new conditions war was no longer a possible method of international dealing. The thing lay upon the surface. The idea of a League of Nations sustaining a Supreme World Court to supersede the arbitrament of war, did not so much arise at any particular point as break out simultaneously wherever there were intelligent men.

Now what was this change in conditions that had confronted mankind with the perplexing necessity of abandoning war? For perplexing it certainly is. War has been a ruling and constructive idea in all human societies up to the present time; few will be found to deny it. Political institutions have very largely developed in relation to the idea of war; defence and aggression have shaped the outer form of every state in the world, just as co-operation sustained by compulsion has shaped its inner organization. And if abruptly man determines to give up the waging of war, he may find that this determination involves the most extensive and penetrating modifications of political and social conceptions that do not at the first glance betray any direct connection with belligerent activities at all.

It is to the general problem arising out of this consideration, that this and the three following essays will be addressed; the question: What else has to go if war is to go out of human life? and the problem of what has to be done if it is to be banished and barred out for ever from the future experiences of our race. For let us face the truth in this matter; the abolition of war is no casting of ancient, barbaric, and now obsolete traditions, no easy and natural progressive step; the abolition of war, if it can be brought about, will be a reversal not only of the general method of human life hitherto but of the general method of nature, the method, that is, of conflict and survival. It will be a new phase in the history of life, and not simply an incident in the history of man. These brief essays will attempt to present something like the true dimensions of the task before mankind if war is indeed to be superseded, and to show that the project of abolishing war by the occasional meeting of some Council of a League of Nations or the like, is, in itself, about as likely to succeed as a proposal to abolish thirst, hunger, and death by a short legislative act.

Let us first examine the change in the conditions of human life that has altered war from a normal aspect of the conflict for existence of human societies into a terror and a threat for the entire species. The change is essentially a change in the amount of power available for human purposes, and more particularly in the amount of material power that can be controlled by one individual. Human society up to a couple of centuries ago was essentially a man-power and horse-power system. There was in addition a certain limited use of water power and wind power, but that was not on a scale to affect the general truth of the proposition. The first intimation of the great change began seven centuries ago with the appearance of explosives. In the thirteenth century the Mongols made a very effective military use of the Chinese discovery of gunpowder. They conquered most of the known world, and their introduction of a low-grade explosive in warfare rapidly destroyed the immunity of castles and walled cities, abolished knighthood, and utterly wrecked and devastated the irrigation system of Mesopotamia, which had been a populous and civilized region since before the beginnings of history. But the restricted metallurgical knowledge of the time set definite limits to the size and range of cannon. It was only with the nineteenth century that the large scale production of cast steel and the growth of chemical knowledge made the military use of a variety of explosives practicable. The systematic extension of human power began in the eighteenth century with the utilization of steam and coal. That opened a crescendo of invention and discovery which thrust rapidly increasing quantities of material energy into men's hands. Even now that crescendo may not have reached its climax.

We need not rehearse here the familiar story of the abolition of distance that ensued; how the radiogram and the telegram have made every event of importance a simultaneous event for the minds of everyone in the world, how journeys which formerly took months or weeks now take days or hours, nor how printing and paper have made possible a universally informed community,

and so forth. Nor will we describe the effect of
these things upon warfare. The point that con-
cerns us here is this, that before this age of discovery, communities had fought and struggled
with each other much as naughty children might
do in a crowded nursery, *within the measure of
their strength.* They had hurt and impoverished
each other, but they had rarely destroyed each
other completely. Their squabbles may have been
distressing, but they were tolerable. It is even
possible to regard these former wars as healthy,
hardening and invigorating conflicts. But into
this nursery has come Science, and has put into
the fists of these children razor blades with poison
on them, bombs of frightful explosive, corrosive
fluids and the like. The comparatively harmless
conflicts of these infants are suddenly fraught with
quite terrific possibilities, and it is only a question
of sooner or later before the nursery becomes a
heap of corpses or is blown to smithereens. A
real nursery invaded by a reckless person dis-
tributing such gifts, would be promptly saved by
the intervention of the nurse; but humanity has
no nurse but its own poor wisdom. And whether
that poor wisdom can rise to the pitch of effectual
intervention is the most fundamental problem in
mundane affairs at the present time.

The deadly gifts continue. There was a steady
increase in the frightfulness and destructiveness
of belligerence from 1914 up to the beginning of
1918, when shortage of material and energy

checked the process; and since the armistice there has been an industrious development of military science. The next well-organized war, we are assured, will be far more swift and extensive in its destruction—more particularly of the civilian population. Armies will advance no longer along roads but extended in line, with heavy tank transport which will plough up the entire surface of the land they traverse; aerial bombing, with bombs each capable of destroying a small town, will be practicable a thousand miles beyond the military front, and the seas will be swept clear of shipping by mines and submarine activities. There will be no distinction between combatants and non-combatants, because every able-bodied citizen, male or female, is a potential producer of food and munitions; and probably the safest, and certainly the best supplied shelters in the universal cataclysm, will be the carefully buried, sand-bagged, and camouflaged general-headquarters of the contending armies. There military gentlemen of limited outlook and high professional training will, in comparative security, achieve destruction beyond their understanding. The hard logic of war which gives victory always to the most energetic and destructive combatant, will turn warfare more and more from mere operations for loot or conquest or predominance into operations for the conclusive destruction of the antagonists. A relentless thrust towards strenuousness is a characteristic of belligerent conditions. War is war, and vehemence is in its nature. You must

hit always as hard as you can. Offensive and
counter-offensive methods continue to prevail over
merely defensive ones. The victor in the next
great war will be bombed from the air, starved,
and depleted almost as much as the loser. His
victory will be no easy one; it will be a triumph
of the exhausted and dying over the dead.

It has been argued that such highly organized
and long prepared warfare as the world saw in
1914-18 is not likely to recur again for a considerable time because of the shock inflicted by it upon
social stability. There may be spasmodic wars
with improvised and scanty supplies, these super-
ficially more hopeful critics admit, but there remain no communities now so stable and so sure of
their people as to prepare and wage again a fully
elaborated scientific war. But this view implies
no happier outlook for mankind. It amounts to
this, that so long as men remain disordered and
impoverished they will not rise again to the full
height of scientific war. But manifestly this will
only be for as long as they remain disordered and
impoverished. When they recover they will recover to repeat again their former disaster with
whatever modern improvements and intensifica-
tions the ingenuity of the intervening time may
have devised. This new phase of disorder, conflict,
and social unravelling upon which we have entered, this phase of decline due to the enhanced
and increasing powers for waste and destruction
in mankind, is bound, therefore, to continue so
long as the divisions based upon ancient ideas of

conflict remain; and if for a time the decadence seems to be arrested, it will only be to accumulate under the influence of those ideas a fresh war storm sufficiently destructive and disorganizing to restore the decadent process.

Unless mankind can readjust its political and social ideas to this essential new fact of its enormously enlarged powers, unless it can eliminate or control its pugnacity, no other prospect seems open to us but decadence, at least to such a level of barbarism as to lose and forget again all the scientific and industrial achievements of our present age. Then, with its powers shrunken to their former puny scale, our race may recover some sort of balance between the injuries and advantages of conflict. Or, since our decadent species may have less vitality and vigour than it had in its primitive phases, it may dwindle and fade out altogether before some emboldened animal antagonist, or through some world-wide disease brought to it perhaps by rats and dogs and insects and what not, who may be destined to be heirs to the rusting and mouldering ruins of the cities and ports and ways and bridges of to-day.

Only one alternative to some such retrogression seems possible, and that is the conscious, systematic reconstruction of human society to avert it. The world has been brought into one community, and the human mind and will may be able to recognize and adapt itself to this fact—in time. Men, as a race, may succeed in turning their backs upon the method of warfare and the methods of conflict and in embarking upon an immense world-wide effort of co-operation and mutual toleration and salvage. They may have the vigour to abandon their age-long attempt to live in separate sovereign states, and to grapple with and master the now quite destructive force that traditional hostility has become, and bring their affairs together under one law and one peace. These new vast powers over nature which have been given to them, and which will certainly be their destruction if their purposes remain divergent and conflicting, will then be the means by which they may set up a new order of as yet scarcely imaginable interest and happiness and achievement. But is our race capable of such an effort, such a complete reversal of its instinctive and traditional impulses? Can we find premonitions of any such bold and revolutionary adaptations as these, in the mental and political life of to-day? How far are we, reader and writer, for example, working for these large new securities? Do we even keep them steadfastly in our minds? How is it with the people around us? Are not we and they and all the race still just as much adrift in the current of circumstances as we were before 1914? Without a great effort on our part (or on someone's part) that current which swirled our kind into a sunshine of hope and opportunity for a while will carry our race on surely and inexorably to fresh wars, to shortages, hunger, miseries, and social débâcles, at last either to complete extinction or to a degradation beyond our present understanding.

§ 2

The urgent need for a great creative effort has become apparent in the affairs of mankind. It is manifest that unless some unity of purpose can be achieved in the world, unless the ever more violent and disastrous incidence of war can be averted, unless some common control can be imposed on the headlong waste of man's limited inheritance of coal, oil, and moral energy that is now going on, the history of humanity must presently culminate in some sort of disaster, repeating and exaggerating the disaster of the great war, producing chaotic social conditions, and going on thereafter in a degenerative process towards extinction. So much all reasonable men seem now prepared to admit. But upon the question of how and in what form a unity of purpose and a common control of human affairs is to be established, there is still a great and lamentable diversity of opinion and, as a consequence, an enfeeblement and wasteful dispersal of will. At present nothing has been produced but the manifestly quite inadequate League of Nations at Geneva, and a number of generally very vague movements for a world law, world disarmament, and the like, among the intellectuals of the various civilized countries of the world.

13

The common failings of all these initiatives are a sort of genteel timidity and a defective sense of the scale of the enterprise before us. A neglect of the importance of scale is one of the gravest faults of contemporary education. Because a world-wide political organ is needed, it does not follow that a so-called League of Nations without representative sanctions, military forces, or authority of any kind, a League from which large sections of the world are excluded altogether, is any contribution to that need. People have a way of saying it is better than nothing. But it may be worse than nothing. It may create a feeling of disillusionment about world-unifying efforts. If a mad elephant were loose in one's garden, it would be an excellent thing to give one's gardener a gun. But it would have to be an adequate gun, an elephant gun. To give him a small rook-rifle and tell him it was better than nothing, and encourage him to face the elephant with that in his hand, would be the directest way of getting rid not of the elephant but of the gardener.

It is, if people will but think steadfastly, inconceivable that there should be any world control without a merger of sovereignty, but the framers of these early tentatives towards world unity have lacked the courage of frankness in this respect. They have been afraid of outbreaks of bawling patriotism, and they have tried to believe, and to make others believe, that they contemplate nothing more than a league of nations, when in reality they contemplate a subordination of nations and administrations to one common law and rule. The elementary necessity of giving the council of any world-peace organization, which is to be more than a sentimental international gesture, not only a complete knowledge but an effective control of all the military resources and organizations in the world, appalled them. They did not even ask for such a control. The frowning solidity of existing things was too much for them. They wanted to change them, but when it came to laying hands on them—No! They decided to leave them alone. They wanted a new world—and it is to contain just the same things as the old.

But are these intellectuals right in their estimate of the common man? Is he such a shallow and vehement fool as they seem to believe? Is he so patriotic as they make out? If mankind is to be saved from destruction there must be a world control; a world control means a world government, it is only another name for it, and manifestly that government must have a navy that will supersede the British navy, artillery that will supersede the French artillery, air forces superseding all existing air forces, and so forth. For many flags there must be one sovereign flag; *orbis terrarum*. Unless a world control amounts to that it will be ridiculous, just as a judge supported by two or three unarmed policemen, a newspaper reporter and the court chaplain, proposing to enforce his decisions in a court packed with the heavily armed friends of the plaintiff and defendant would be ridiculous. But the common man is supposed to

be so blindly and incurably set upon his British
navy or his French army, or whatever his pet
national instrument of violence may be, that it is
held to be impossible to supersede these beloved
and adored forces. If that is so, then a world law
is impossible, and the wisest course before us is
to snatch such small happiness as we may hope to
do and leave the mad elephant to work its will in
the garden.

But is it so? If the mass of common men are
incurably patriotic and belligerent why is there a
note of querulous exhortation in nearly all
patriotic literature? Why, for instance, is Mr.
Rudyard Kipling's "History of England" so full
of goading and scolding? And very significant indeed to any student of the human outlook was the
world response to President Wilson's advocacy of
the League of Nations idea, in its first phase in
1918, before the weakening off and disillusionment
of the Versailles conference. Just for a little while
it seemed that President Wilson stood for a new
order of things in the world, that he had the
wisdom and will and power to break the net of
hatreds and nationalisms and diplomacies in which
the Old World was entangled. And while he
seemed to be capable of that, while he promised
most in the way of change and national control,
then it was that he found his utmost support in
every country in the world. In the latter half of
1918 there was scarcely a country anywhere in
which one could not have found men ready to die
for President Wilson. A great hopefulness was

manifest in the world. It faded, it faded very rapidly again. But that brief wave of enthusiasm, which set minds astir with the same great idea of one peace of justice throughout the earth in China and Bokhara and the Indian bazaars, in Iceland and Basutoland and Ireland and Morocco, was indeed a fact perhaps more memorable in history even than the great war itself. It displayed a possibility of the simultaneous operation of the same general ideas throughout the world quite beyond any previous experience. It demonstrated that the generality of men are as capable of being cosmopolitan and pacifist as they are of being patriotic and belligerent. Both moods are extensions and exaltations beyond the everyday life, which itself is neither one thing nor the other. And both are transitory moods, responses to external suggestion.

It is to that first wave of popular feeling for a world law transcending and moving counter to all contemporary diplomacies, and not to the timid legalism of the framers of the first schemes for a League of Nations that we must look, if we are to hope at all for the establishment of a new order in human affairs. It is upon the spirit of that transitory response to the transitory greatness of President Wilson that we have to seize; we have to lay hold of that, to recall it and confirm it and enlarge and strengthen it, to make it a flux of patriotisms and a creator of new loyalties and devotions, and out of the dead dust of our present institutions to build up for it and animate with it the body of a true world state.

We have already stated the clear necessity, if mankind is not to perish by the hypertrophy of warfare, for the establishment of an armed and strong world law. Here in this spirit that has already gleamed upon the world is the possible force to create and sustain such a world law What is it that intervenes between the universal human need and its satisfaction? Why, since there are overwhelming reasons for it and a widespread disposition for it, is there no world-wide creative effort afoot now in which men and women by the million are participating—and participating with all their hearts? Why is it that, except for the weak gestures of the Geneva League of Nations and a little writing of books and articles, a little pamphleteering, some scattered committee activities on the part of people chiefly of the busybody class, an occasional speech and a diminishing volume of talk and allusion, no attempts are apparent to stay the plain drift of human society towards new conflicts and the sluices of final disaster?

The answer to that Why, probes deep into the question of human motives.

It must be because we are all creatures of our immediate surroundings, because our minds and energies are chiefly occupied by the affairs of every day, because we are all chiefly living our own lives, and very few of us, except by a kind of unconscious contribution, the life of mankind.

In moments of mental activity, in the study or in contemplation, we may rise to a sense of the dangers and needs of human destiny, but it is only a few minds and characters of prophetic quality that, without elaborate artificial assistance, seem able to keep hold upon and guide their lives by such relatively gigantic considerations. The generality of men and women, so far as their natural disposition goes, are scarcely more capable of apprehending and consciously serving the human future than a van full of well-fed rabbits would be of grasping the fact that their van was running smoothly and steadily down an inclined plane into the sea. It is only as the result of considerable educational effort and against considerable resistance that our minds are brought to a broader view. In every age for many thousands of years men of exceptionl vision have spent their lives in passionate efforts to bring us ordinary men into some relation of response and service to the greater issues of life. It is these pioneers of vision who have given the world its religions and its philosophical cults, its loyalties and observances; and who have imposed ideas of greatness and duty on their fellows. In every age the ordinary man has submitted reluctantly to such teachings, has made his peculiar compromises with them, has reduced them as far as possible to formula and formality, and got back as rapidly as possible to the eating and drinking and desire, the personal spites and rivalries and glories which constitute his reality. The mass of men to-day do not seem to care, nor

want to care, whither the political and social institutions to which they are accustomed are taking
them. Such considerations overstrain us. And it
is only by the extremest effort of those who are
capable of a sense of racial danger and duty that
the collective energies of men can ever be gathered
together and organized and orientated towards
the common good. To nearly all men and women,
unless they are in the vein for it, such discussion
as this in these essays does not appeal as being
right or wrong; it does not really interest them,
rather it worries them; and for the most part they
would be glad to disregard it as completely as a
lecture on wheels and gravitation and the physio-
logical consequences of prolonged submergence
would be disregarded by those rabbits in the van.

But man is a creature very different in his
nature from a rabbit, and if he is less instinctively
social, he is much more consciously social. Chief
among his differences must be the presence of
those tendencies which we call conscience, that
haunting craving to be really right and to do the
really right thing which is the basis of the moral
and perhaps also of most of the religious life. In
this lies our hope for mankind. Man hates to be
put right, and yet also he wants to be right. He
is a creature divided against himself, seeking both
to preserve and to overcome his egotism. It is
upon the presence of the latter strand in man's
complex make-up that we must rest our hopes of
a developing will for the world state which will

gradually gather together and direct into a
massive constructive effort the now quite dis-
persed chaotic and traditional activities of
men.

As we have examined this problem it has become clear that the task of bringing about that
consolidated world state which is necessary to prevent the decline and decay of mankind is not
primarily one for the diplomatists and lawyers
and politicians at all. It is an educational one.
It is a moral based on an intellectual reconstruction. The task immediately before mankind is to
find release from the contentious loyalties and
hostilities of the past which make collective world-
wide action impossible at the present time, in a
world-wide common vision of the history and destinies of the race. On that as a basis, and on that
alone, can a world control be organized and main-
tained. The effort demanded from mankind,
therefore, is primarily and essentially a bold reconstruction of the outlook upon life of hundreds
of millions of minds. The idea of a world commonweal has to be established as the criterion of
political institutions, and also as the criterion of
general conduct in hundreds of millions of brains.
It has to dominate education everywhere in the
world. When that end is achieved, then the world
state will be achieved, and it can be achieved in
no other way. And unless that world state can
be achieved, it would seem that the outlook before
mankind is a continuance of disorder and of more

and more destructive and wasteful conflicts, a steady process of violence, decadence, and misery towards extinction, or towards modifications of our type altogether beyond our present understanding and sympathy.

3

In framing an estimate of the human future two leading facts are dominant. The first is the plain necessity for a political reorganization of the world as a unity, to save our race from the social disintegration and complete physical destruction which war, under modern conditions, must ultimately entail, and the second is the manifest absence of any sufficient will in the general mass of mankind at the present time to make such a reorganization possible. There appear to be the factors of such a will in men, but they are for the most part unawakened, or they are unorganized and ineffective. And there is a very curious incapacity to grasp the reality of the human situation, a real resistance to seeing things as they are —for man is an effort-shirking animal—which greatly impedes the development of such a will. Failing the operation of such a sufficient will, human affairs are being directed by use and wont, by tradition and accidental deflections. Mankind, after the tragic concussion of the great war, seems now to be drifting again towards new and probably more disastrous concussions.

The catastrophe of the great war did more or less completely awaken a certain limited number of intelligent people to the need of some general

control replacing this ancient traditional driftage
of events. But they shrank from the great impli-
cations of such a world control. The only practicable way to achieve a general control in the face
of existing governments, institutions and prejudices, interested obstruction and the common disregard, is by extending this awakening to great
masses of people. This means an unprecedented
educational effort, an appeal to men's intelligence
and men's imagination such as the world has never
seen before. Is it possible to rationalize the at
present chaotic will of mankind? That possibility,
if it is a possibility, is the most important thing in
contemporary human affairs.

We are asking here for an immense thing, for
a change of ideas, a vast enlargement of ideas, and
for something very like a change of heart in
hundreds of millions of human beings. But then
we are dealing with the fate of the entire species.
We are discussing the prevention of wars, dis-
orders, shortages, famines and miseries for centuries ahead. The initial capital we have to go
upon is as yet no more than the aroused understanding and conscience of a few thousands, at
most of a few score thousands of people. Can so
little a leaven leaven so great a lump? Is a response to this appeal latent in the masses of mankind? Is there anything in history to justify hope
for so gigantic a mental turnover in our race?

A consideration of the spread of Christianity
in the first four centuries A.D. or of the spread
of Islam in the seventh century will, we believe,

support a reasonable hope that such a change in the minds of men, whatever else it may be, is a practicable change, that it can be done and that it may even probably be done. Consider our two instances. The propagandas of those two great religions changed and changed for ever the political and social outlook over vast areas of the world's surface. Yet while the stir for world unity begins now simultaneously in many countries and many groups of people, those two propagandas each radiated from one single centre and were in the first instance the teachings of single individuals; and while to-day we can deal with great reading populations and can reach them by press and printed matter, by a universal distribution of books, by great lecturing organizations and the like, those earlier great changes in human thought were achieved mainly by word of mouth and by crabbed manuscripts, painfully copied and passed slowly from hand to hand. So far it is only the trader who has made any effectual use of the vast facilities the modern world has produced for conveying a statement simultaneously to great numbers of people at a distance. The world of thought still hesitates to use the means of power that now exist for it. History and political philosophy in the modern world are like bashful dons at a dinner party; they crumble their bread and talk in undertones and clever allusions to their nearest neighbour, abashed at the thought of addressing the whole table. But in a world where Mars can reach out in a single night and smite a city a thousand miles away, we cannot suffer wisdom to hesitate in an inaudible gentility. The knowledge and vision that is good enough for the best of us is good enough for all. This gospel of human brotherhood and a common law and rule for all mankind, the attempt to meet this urgent necessity of a common control of human affairs, which indeed is no new religion but only an attempt to realize practically the common teaching of all the established religions of the world, has to speak with dominating voice everywhere between the poles and round about the world.

And it must become part of the universal education. It must speak through the school and university. It is too often forgotten, in America, perhaps, even more than in Europe, that education exists for the community, and for the individual only so far as it makes him a sufficient member of the community. The chief end of education is to subjugate and sublimate for the collective purposes of our kind the savage egotism we inherit. Every school, every college, teaches directly and still more by implication, relationship to a community and devotion to a community. In too many cases that community we let our schools and colleges teach to our children is an extremely narrow one; it is the community of a sect, of a class, or of an intolerant, greedy and unrighteous nationalism. Schools have increased greatly in numbers throughout the world during the last century, but there has been little or no growth in the conception of education in schools. Education has been extended, but it has not been developed. If man is to be saved from self-destruction by the organization of a world community, there must be a broadening of the reference of the teaching in the schools of all the world to that community of the world. World-wide educational development and reform are the necessary preparations for and the necessary accompaniments of a political reconstruction of the world. The two are the right and left hands of the same thing. Neither can effect much without the other.

Now it is manifest that this reorganization of the world's affairs and of the world's education which we hold to be imperatively dictated by the change in warfare, communications and other conditions of human life brought about by scientific discovery during 'he last hundred years, carries with it a practical repudiation of the claims of every existing sovereign government in the world to be final and sovereign, to be anything more than provisional and replaceable. There is the difficulty that has checked hundreds of men after their first step towards this work for a universal peace. It involves, it cannot but involve, a revision of their habitual allegiances. At best existing governments are to be regarded as local trustees and caretakers for the coming human commonweal. If they are not that, then they are necessarily obstructive and antagonistic. But few rulers, few governments, few officials, will have the greatness of mind to recognize and admit this plain reality. By a kind of necessity they

force upon their subjects and publics a conflict of
loyalties. The feeble driftage of human affairs
from one base or greedy arrangement or cowardly
evasion to another, since the Armistice of 1918,
is very largely due to the obstinate determination
of those who are in positions of authority and
responsibility to ignore the plain teachings of the
great war and its sequelæ. They are resisting
adjustments; their minds are fighting against the
sacrifices of pride and authority that a full recognition of their subordination to the world commonweal will involve. They are prepared, it
would seem, to fight against the work of human
salvation basely and persistently, whenever their
accustomed importance is threatened.

Even in the schools and in the world of thought
the established thing will make its unrighteous
fight for life. The dull and the dishonest in high
places will suppress these greater ideas when they
can, and ignore when they dare not suppress. It
seems too much to hope for that there should be
any willingness on the part of any established authority to admit its obsolescence and prepare the
way for its merger in a world authority. It is not
creative minds that produce revolutions, but the
obstinate conservatism of established authority.
It is the blank refusal to accept the idea of an
orderly evolution towards new things that gives a
revolutionary quality to every constructive proposal. The huge task of political and educational
reconstruction which is needed to arrest the present drift of human affairs towards catastrophe,

must bē achieved, if it is to be achieved at all,
mainly by voluntary and unofficial effort; and for
the most part in the teeth of official opposition.

There are one or two existing states to which
men have looked for some open recognition of
their duty to mankind as a whole, and of the
necessarily provisional nature of their contemporary constitutions. The United States of America
constitute a political system, profoundly different
in its origin and in its spirit, from any old-world
state; it was felt that here at least might be an
evolutionary state; and in the palmy days of
President Wilson it did seem for a brief interval
as if the New World was indeed coming to the
rescue of the old, as if America was to play the
rôle of a propagandist continent, bringing its
ideas of equality and freedom, and extending the
spirit of its union to all the nations of the earth.
From that expectation, the world opinion is now
in a state of excessive and unreasonable recoil.
President Wilson fell away from his first intima-
tions of that world-wide federal embrace, his mind
and will were submerged by the clamour of contending patriotisms and the subtle expedients of
old-world diplomacy in Paris; but American acces-
sibility to the idea of a federalized world neither
began with him nor will it end with his failure.
America is still a hopeful laboratory of world-
unifying thought. A long string of arbitration
treaties stands to the credit of America, and a
series of developing Pan-American projects, point-
ing clearly to at least a continental synthesis

within a measurable time. There has been, and there still is, a better understanding of, and a greater receptivity to, ideas of international synthesis in America than in any European state.

And the British Empire, which, according to many of its liberal apologists is already a league of nations, linked together in a mutually advantageous peace, to that too men have looked for some movement of adaptation to this greater synthesis which is the world's pre-eminent need. But so far the British Empire has failed to respond to such expectations. The war has left it strained and bruised and with its affairs very much in the grip of the military class, the most illiterate and dangerous class in the community. They have done, perhaps, irreparable mischief to the peace of the empire in Ireland, India and Egypt, and they have made the claim of the British system to be an exemplary unification of dissimilar peoples seem now to many people incurably absurd. It is a great misfortune for mankind that the British Empire, which played so sturdy and central a part in the great war, could at its close achieve no splendid and helpful gesture towards a generous reconstruction.

Since the armistice there has been an extraordinary opportunity for the British monarchy to have displayed a sense of the new occasions before the world, and to have led the way towards the efforts and renunciations of an international renascence. It could have taken up a lead that the President of the United States had initiated and relinquished; it could have used its peculiar position to make an unexampled appeal to the whole world. It could have created a new epoch in history. The Prince of Wales has been touring the world-wide dominions of which, some day, he is to be the crowned head. He has received addresses, visited sights, been entertained, shaken hands with scores of thousands of people and submitted himself to the eager, yet unpenetrating gaze of vast multitudes. His smallest acts have been observed with premeditated admiration, his lightest words recorded. He is not now a boy; he saw something of the great war, even if his exalted position denied him any large share of its severer hardships and dangers; he cannot be blind to the general posture of the world's affairs. Here, surely, was a chance of saying something that would be heard from end to end of the earth, something kingly and great-minded. Here was the occasion for a fine restatement of the obligations and duties of empire. But from first to last the prince has said nothing to quicken the imaginations of the multitude of his future subjects to the gigantic possibilities of these times, nothing to reassure the foreign observer that the British Empire embodies anything more than the colossal national egotism and impenetrable self-satisfaction of the British peoples. "Here we are," said the old order in those demonstrations, "and here we mean to stick. Just as we have been, so we remain. British!—we are Bourbons." These smiling tours of the Prince of Wales in these

years of shortage, stress, and insecurity, constitute a propaganda of inanity unparalleled in the
world's history.

Nor do we find in the nominal rulers and official
representatives of other countries any clear ad-
mission of the necessity for a great and fundamental change in the scope and spirit of government. These official and ruling people, more than
any other people, are under the sway of that life
of use and wont which dominates us all. They are
often trained to their positions, or they have won
their way to their positions of authority through
a career of political activities which amounts to a
training. And that training is not a training in
enterprise and change; it is a training in sticking
tight and getting back to precedent. We can expect nothing from them. We shall be lucky if
the resistance of the administrative side of existing states to the conception of a world commonweal is merely passive. There is little or no prospect of any existing governing system, unless it
be such a federal system as Switzerland or the
United States, passing directly and without extensive internal changes into combination with other
sovereign powers as part of a sovereign world
system. At some point the independent states
will as systems resist, and unless an overwhelming
world conscience for the world state has been
brought into being and surrounds them with an
understanding watchfulness, and invades the consciences of their supporters and so weakens their

resisting power, they will resist violently and disastrously. But it will be an incoherent resistance because the very nature of the sovereign states of to-day is incoherence. There can be no worldwide combination of sovereign states to resist the world state, because that would be to create the world state in the attempt to defeat it.

4

In the three preceding essays an attempt has
been made to state the pass at which mankind has
arrived, the dangers and mischiefs that threaten
our race, and the need there is and the opportunities there are for a strenuous attempt to end
the age-long bickerings of nations and empires
and establish one community of law and effort
throughout the whole world. Stress has been laid
chiefly upon the monstrous evils and disasters a
continuation of our present divisions, our nationalisms and imperialisms and the like, will certainly
entail. These considerations of evil, however, are
only the negative argument for this creative effort; they have been thrust forward because war,
disorder, insufficiency, and the ill health, the part-
ings, deprivations, boredom and unhappiness that
arise out of these things are well within our experience and entirely credible; the positive argument
for a world order demands at once more faith and
imagination.

Given a world law and world security, a release
from the net of bickering frontiers, world-wide
freedom of movement, and world-wide fellowship,
a thousand good things that are now beyond hope
or dreaming would come into the ordinary life.
The whole world would be our habitation, and the

energies of men, released from their preoccupation with contention, would go more and more abundantly into the accumulation and application of scientific knowledge, that is to say into the increase of mental and bodily health, of human power, of interest and happiness. Even to-day the most delightful possibilities stand waiting, inaccessible to nearly all of us because of the general insecurity, distrust and anger. Flying, in a world safely united in peace, could take us now to the ends of the earth smoothly, securely through the sweet upper air, in five or six days. In two or three years there could again be abundance of food and pleasant clothing for everyone throughout the whole world. Men could be destroying their slums and pestilential habitations and rebuilding spacious and beautiful cities. Given only peace and confidence and union we could double our yearly production of all that makes life desirable and still double our leisure for thought and growth. We could live in a universal palace and make the whole globe our garden and playground.

But these are not considerations that sway people to effort. Fear and hate, not hope and desire, have been hitherto the effective spurs for men. The most popular religions are those which hold out the widest hopes of damnation. Our lives are lives of use and wont, we distrust the promise of delightful experience and achievements beyond our accustomed ways; it offends our self-satisfaction even to regard them as possibilities; we do not like the implied cheapening of familiar things. We are all ready to sneer at "Utopias," as elderly invalids sneer at the buoyant hopes of youth and do their best to think them sure of frustration. The aged and disillusioned profess a keen appreciation of the bath chair and the homely spoonful of medicine, and pity a crudity that misses the fine quality of those ripe established things. Most people are quite ready to dismiss the promise of a full free life for all mankind with a sneer. That would rob the world of romance, they say, the romance of passport offices, custom houses, shortages of food, endless petty deprivations, slums, pestilence, under-educated stunted children, youths dying in heaps in muddy trenches, an almost universal lack of vitality, and all the picturesque eventfulness of contemporary conditions. So that we have not dwelt here upon the life-giving aspect of a possible world-state, but only on its life-saving aspects. We have not argued that our present life of use and wont could be replaced by an infinitely better way of living. We have rather pointed out that if things continue to drift as they are doing, the present life of use and wont will become intolerably insecure. It is the thought of the large bombing aeroplane and not the hope of swift travelling across the sky that will move the generality of men, if they are to be moved at all, towards a world peace.

But whether the lever that moves them is desire or fear the majority of men, unless the species is to perish, must be brought within a measurable time to an understanding of, and a will for, a single world government. And since at first existing institutions, established traditions, educational organizations and the like, will all be passively if not actively resistant to the spread of this saving idea, and much more so to any attempts to realize this saving idea, there remains nothing for us to look to, at the present time, for the first organization of this immense effort of mental reversal, but the zeal and devotion and self-sacrifice of convinced individuals. The world state must begin; it can only begin, as a propagandist cult, or as a group of propagandist cults, to which men and women must give themselves and their energies, regardless of the consequences to themselves. Laying the foundations of a world state upon a site already occupied by a muddle of buildings is an undertaking which will almost necessarily bring its votaries into conflict with established authority and current sentiment; they will have to face the possibility of lives of conflict, misunderstanding, much thankless exertion; they must count on little honour and considerable active dislike; and they will have to find what consolation they can in the interest of the conflict itself and in the thought of a world, made at last by such efforts as theirs, peaceful and secure and vigorous, a world they can never hope to see. So stated it seems a bad bargain that the worker for the world-state is invited to make, yet the world has never lacked people prepared to make such a bargain and they will not fail it now. There are

worse things than conflict without manifest victory and effort without apparent reward. To the
finer kind of mind it is infinitely more tragic and
distressing to find that existence bears a foolish
aimless face. Many people, tormented by the dis-
content of conscience, and wanting, more than they
can ever want any satisfaction, some satisfying
rule of life, some criterion of conduct, will find in
this cult of the world-state just that sustaining
reality they need. And their number will grow.
Because it is a practical and reasonable shape for
a life, arising naturally out of a proper understanding of history and physical science, and em-
bodying in a unifying plan the teaching of all the
great religions of the world. It comes to us not
to destroy but to fulfil.

The activities of a cult which set itself to bring
about the world-state would at first be propagandist, they would be intellectual and educational, and only as a sufficient mass of opinion and
will had accumulated would they become to a pre-
dominant extent politically constructive. Such a
cult must direct itself particularly to the teaching
of the young. So far the propaganda for a world
law, the League of Nations propaganda, since it
has sought immediate political results, has been
addressed almost entirely to adults; and as a consequence it has had to adapt itself as far as possible to their preconceptions about the history and
outlook of their own nationality, and to the general absence as yet in the world of any vision of
the welfare of mankind as one whole. It is be-

cause of this acceptance of current adult ideas about patriotism and nationality that the movement has adopted the unsatisfactory phrase, a League of Nations, when what is contemplated is much more than a league and a very considerable subordination of national sovereignty. And a large share in the current ineffectiveness of the League of Nations is evidently due to the fact that men interpret the phrase and the proposition of the League of Nations differently in accordance with the different fundamental historical ideas they possess, ideas that propaganda has hitherto left unassailed. The worker for the world-state will look further and plough deeper. It is these fundamental ideas which are the vitally important objective of a world-unifying movement, and they can only be brought into that world-wide uniformity which is essential to the enduring peace of mankind, by teaching children throughout all the earth the common history of their kind, and so directing their attention to the common future of their descendants. The driving force that makes either war or peace is engendered where the young are taught. The teacher, whether mother, priest, or schoolmaster, is the real maker of history; rulers, statesmen and soldiers do but work out the possibilities of co-operation or conflict the teacher creates. This is no rhetorical flourish; it is a sober fact. The politicians and masses of our time dance on the wires of their early education.

Teaching then is the initial and decisive factor

in the future of mankind, and the first duty of everyone who has the ability and opportunity, is to teach, or to subserve the teaching of, the true history of mankind and of the possibilities of this vision of a single world-state that history opens out to us. Men and women can help the spread of the saving doctrine in a thousand various ways; for it is not only in homes and schools that minds are shaped. They can print and publish books, endow schools and teaching, organize the distribution of literature, insist upon the proper instruction of children in world-wide charity and fellowship, fight against every sort of suppression or restrictive control of right education, bring pressure through political and social channels upon every teaching organization to teach history aright, sustain missions and a new sort of missionary, the missionaries to all mankind of knowledge and the idea of one world civilization and one world community; they can promote and help the progress of historical and ethnological and political science, they can set their faces against every campaign of hate, racial suspicion, and patriotic falsehood, they can refuse, they are bound to refuse, obedience to any public authority which oppresses and embitters class against class, race against race, and people against people. A belligerent government as such, they can refuse to obey; and they can refuse to help or suffer any military preparations that are not directed wholly and plainly to preserving the peace of the world. This is the plain duty of every honest man to-day,

to judge his magistrate before he obeys him, and
to render unto Cæsar nothing that he owes to God
and mankind. And those who are awakened to
the full significance of the vast creative effort
now before mankind will set themselves particularly to revise the common moral judgment upon
many acts and methods of living that obstruct
the way of the world-state. Blatant, aggressive
patriotism and the incitements against foreign
peoples that usually go with it, are just as crimi-
nal and far more injurious to our race than, for
example, indecent provocations and open incitements to sexual vice; they produce a much beast-
lier and crueller state of mind, and they deserve
at least an equal condemnation. Yet you will find
even priests and clergymen to-day rousing the
war passions of their flocks and preaching conflict from the very steps of the altar.

So far the movement towards a world-state has
lacked any driving power of passion. We have
been passing through a phase of intellectual revision. The idea of a world unity and brotherhood has come back again into the world almost
apologetically, deferentially, asking for the kind
words of successful politicians and for a gesture
of patronage from kings. Yet this demand for
one world-empire of righteousness was inherent in
the teachings of Buddha, it flashed for a little
while behind the sword of Islam, it is the embodi-
ment in earthly affairs of the spirit of Christ. It
is a call to men for service as of right, it is not an
appeal to them that they may refuse, not a voice

that they may disregard. It is too great a thing
to hover for long thus deferentially on the out-
skirts of the active world it has come to save.
To-day the world-state says: "Please listen; make
way for me." To-morrow it will say: "Make
way for me, little people." The day is not remote when disregardful "patriotic" men hector-
ing in the crowd will be twisted round perforce to
the light they refuse to see. First comes the idea
and then slowly the full comprehension of the idea,
comes realization, and with that realization will
come a kindling anger at the vulgarity, the mean-
ness, the greed and baseness and utter stupidity
that refuses to attend to this clear voice, this definite demand of our racial necessity. To-day we
teach, but as understanding grows we must begin
to act. We must put ourselves and our rulers and
our fellow men on trial. We must ask: "What
have you done, and what are you doing to help or
hinder the peace and order of mankind?" A time
will come when a politician who has wilfully made
war and promoted international dissension will be
as sure of the dock and much surer of the noose
than a private homicide. It is not reasonable that
those who gamble with men's lives should not
stake their own. The service of the world-state
calls for much more than passive resistance to
belligerent authorities, for much more than exemplary martyrdoms. It calls for the greater effort
of active interference with mischievous men. "I
will believe in the League of Nations," one man
has written, "when men will fight for it." For

this League of Nations at Geneva, this little corner of Balfourian jobs and gentility, no man would dream of fighting, but for the great state of mankind, men will presently be very ready to fight and, as the thing may go, either to kill or die. Things must come in their order; first the idea, then the kindling of imaginations, then the world-wide battle. We who live in the bleak days after a great crisis, need be no more discouraged by the apparent indifference of the present time than are fields that are ploughed and sown by the wet days of February and the cold indifference of the winds of early March. The ploughing has been done, and the seed is in the ground, and the world-state stirs in a multitude of germinating minds.

II

THE PROJECT OF A WORLD STATE *

In this paper, I want to tell you of the idea that now shapes and dominates my public life—the idea of a world politically united—of a world securely and permanently at peace. And I want to say what I have to say, so far as regards the main argument of it, as accurately and plainly as possible, without any eloquence or flourishes.

When I first planned this paper, I chose as the title "The Utopia of a World State." Well, there is something a little too flimsy and unpracticable about that word Utopia. To most people Utopia conveys the idea of a high-toned political and ethical dream—agreeable and edifying, no doubt, but of no practical value whatever. What I have to talk about this evening is not a bit dreamlike, it is about real dangers and urgent necessities. It is a Project and not a Utopia. It may be a vast and impossible Project. It may be a hopeless Project. But if it fails our Civilization fails. And so I have called this paper not the Utopia but *The Project of a World State*.

There are some things that it is almost impossible to tell without seeming to scream and exag-

* Written originally as a lecture to be delivered in America.

44

gerate, and yet these things may be in reality the soberest matter of fact. I want to say that this civilization in which we are living is tumbling down, and I think tumbling down very fast; that I think rapid enormous efforts will be needed to save it; and that I see no such efforts being made at the present time. I do not know if these words convey any concrete ideas to the reader's mind. There are statements that can open such unfamiliar vistas as to seem devoid of any real practical meaning at all, and this I think may be one of them.

In the past year I have been going about Europe. I have had glimpses of a new phase of this civilization of ours—a new phase that would have sounded like a fantastic dream if one had told about it ten years ago. I have seen a great city that had over two million inhabitants, dying and dying with incredible rapidity. In 1914 I was in the city of St. Petersburg and it seemed as safe and orderly a great city as yours. I went thither in comfortable and punctual trains. I stayed in an hotel as well equipped and managed as any American hotel. I went to dine with and visit households of cultivated people. I walked along streets of brilliantly lit and well-furnished shops. It was, in fact, much the same sort of life that you are living here to-day—a part of our (then) world-wide modern civilization.

I revisited these things last summer. I found such a spectacle of decay that it seems almost impossible to describe it to those who have never

seen the like. Streets with great holes where the
drains had fallen in. Stretches of roadway from
which the wood paving had been torn for fire-
wood. Lampposts that had been knocked over
lying as they were left, without an attempt to set
them up again. Shops and markets deserted and
decayed and ruinous. Not closed shops but aban-
doned shops, as abandoned-looking as an old boot
or an old can by the wayside. The railways falling out of use. A population of half a million
where formerly there had been two. A strangely
homeless city, a city of discomforts and anxieties,
a city of want and ill-health and death. Such was
Petersburg in 1920.

I know there are people who have a quick and
glib explanation of this vast and awe-inspiring
spectacle of a great empire in collapse. They say
it is Bolshevism has caused all this destruction.
But I hope to show here, among other more important things, that Bolshevism is merely a part
of this immense collapse—that the overthrow of a
huge civilized organization needs some more comprehensive explanation than that a little man
named Lenin was able to get from Geneva to
Russia at a particular crisis in Russian history.
And particularly is it to be noted that this immense destruction of civilized life has not been
confined to Russia or to regions under Bolshevik
rule. Austria and Hungary present spectacles
hardly less desolating than Russia. There is a
conspicuous ebb in civilization in Eastern Germany. And even when you come to France and

Italy and Ireland there are cities, townships, whole wide regions, where you can say: This has gone back since 1914 and it is still going back in material prosperity, in health, in social order.

Even in England and Scotland, in Holland and Denmark and Sweden, it is hard to determine whether things are stagnant or moving forward or moving back—they are certainly not going ahead as they were before 1913-14. The feeling in England is rather like the feeling of a man who is not quite sure whether he has caught a slight chill or whether he is in the opening stage of a serious illness.

Now what I want to do here is to theorize about this shadow, this chill and arrest, that seems to have come upon the flourishing and expanding civilization in which all of us were born and reared. I want to put a particular view of what is happening before you, and what it is that we are up against. I want to put before you for your judgment the view that this overstrain and breaking down and stoppage of the great uprush of civilization that has gone on for the past three centuries is due to the same forces and is the logical outcome of the same forces that led to that uprush, to that tremendous expansion of human knowledge and power and life. And that that breaking up is an inevitable thing unless we meet it by a very great effort of a particular kind.

Now the gist of my case is this: That the civilization of the past three centuries has produced a great store of scientific knowledge, and that this scientific knowledge has altered the material scale of human affairs and enormously enlarged the physical range of human activities, but that there has been no adequate adjustment of men's political ideas to the new conditions.

This adjustment is a subtle and a difficult task. It is also a greatly neglected task. And upon the possibility of our making this adjustment depends the issue whether the ebb of civilizing energy, the actual smashing and breaking down of modern civilization, which has already gone very far indeed in Russia and which is going on in most of Eastern and Central Europe, extends to the whole civilized world.

Let me make a very rough and small scale analysis of what is happening to the world to-day. And let us disregard many very important issues and concentrate upon the chief, most typical issue, the revolution in the facilities of locomotion and communication that has occurred to the world and the consequences of that revolution. For the international problem to-day is essentially dependent upon the question of transport and communication—all others are subordinate to that. I shall particularly call your attention to certain wide differences between the American case and the old-world case in this matter.

It is not understood clearly enough at the present time how different is the American international problem from the European international problem, and how inevitable it is that America and Europe should approach international problems from a different angle and in a different spirit. Both lines of thought and experience do, I believe, lead at last to the world state, but they get there by a different route and in a different manner.

The idea that the government of the United States can take its place side by side with the governments of the old world on terms of equality with those governments in order to organize the peace of the world, is, I believe, a mistaken and unworkable idea. I shall argue that the government of the United States and the community of the United States are things different politically and mentally from those of the states of the old world, and that the rôle they are destined to play in the development of a world state of mankind is essentially a distinctive one. And I shall try to show cause for regarding the very noble and splendid project of a world-wide League of Nations that has held the attention of the world for the past three years, as one that is, at once, a little too much for complete American participation, and not sufficient for the urgent needs of Europe. It is not really so practicable and reasonable a proposition as it seemed at first.

The idea of a world state, though it looks a far greater and more difficult project, is, in the long run, a sounder and more hopeful proposition.

Now let me make myself as clear as I can be about the central idea upon which the whole of the arguments in this lecture rests. It is this: forgive me for a repetition—that there has been a complete alteration in the range and power of human activities in the last hundred years. Men can react upon men with a rapidity and at a distance inconceivable a hundred years ago. This is particularly the case with locomotion and methods of communication generally. I will not remind you in any detail of facts with which you are familiar; how that in the time of Napoleon the most rapid travel possible of the great conqueror himself did not average all over as much as four and a half miles an hour. A hundred and seven miles a day for thirteen days—the pace of his rush from Vilna to Paris after the Moscow disaster— was regarded as a triumph of speed. In those days too, it was a marvel that by means of sema- phores it was possible to transmit a short mes- sage from London to Portsmouth in the course of an hour or so.

Since then we have seen a development of teleg- raphy that has at last made news almost simul- taneous about the world, and a steady increase in the rate of travel until, as we worked it out in the Civil Air Transport Committee in London, it is possible, if not at present practicable, to fly from London to Australia, half way round the earth, in about eight days. I say possible, but not prac- ticable, because at present properly surveyed routes, landing grounds and adequate supplies of petrol and spare parts do not exist. Given those things, that journey could be done now in the time I have stated. This tremendous change in the range of human activities involves changes in the conditions of our political life that we are only beginning to work out to their proper consequences to-day.

It is a curious thing that America, which owes most to this acceleration in locomotion, has felt it least. The United States have taken the railway, the river steamboat, the telegraph and so forth as though they were a natural part of their growth. They were not. These things happened to come along just in time to save American unity. The United States of to-day were made first by the river steamboat, and then by the railway. Without these things, the present United States, this vast continental nation, would have been altogether impossible. The westward flow of population would have been far more sluggish. It might never have crossed the great central plains. It took, you will remember, nearly two hundred years for effective settlement to reach from the coast to the Missouri, much less than half-way across the continent. The first state established beyond the river was the steamboat state of Missouri in 1821. But the rest of the distance to the Pacific was done in a few decades.

If we had the resources of the cinema it would be interesting to show a map of North America year by year from 1600 onward, with little dots to represent hundreds of people, each dot a hundred, and stars to represent cities of a hundred thousand people.

For two hundred years you would see that stippling creeping slowly along the coastal districts and navigable waters, spreading still more gradually into Indiana, Kentucky, and so forth. Then somewhere about 1810 would come a change. Things would get more lively along the river courses. The dots would be multiplying and spreading. That would be the steamboat. The pioneer dots would be spreading soon from a number of jumping-off places along the great rivers over Kansas and Nebraska.

Then from about 1830 onward would come the black lines of the railways, and after that the little black dots would not simply creep but run. They would appear now so rapidly, it would be almost as though they were being put on by some sort of spraying machine. And suddenly here and then there would appear the first stars to indicate the first great cities of a hundred thousand people. First one or two and then a multitude of cities—each like a knot in the growing net of the railways.

This is a familiar story. I recall it to you now to enforce this point—that the growth of the United States is a process that has no precedent in the world's history; it is a new kind of occurrence. Such a community could not have come into existence before, and if it had it would, without railways, have certainly dropped to pieces long before now. Without railways or telegraph it would be far easier to administer California from Pekin than from Washington. But this great population of the United States of America has not only grown outrageously; it has kept uniform. Nay, it has become more uniform. The man of

San Francisco is more like the man of New York to-day than the man of Virginia was like the man of New England a century ago. And the process of assimilation goes on unimpeded. The United States is being woven by railway, by telegraph, more and more into one vast human unity, speaking, thinking, and acting harmoniously with itself. Soon aviation will be helping in the work.

Now this great community of the United States is, I repeat, an altogether new thing in history. There have been great empires before with populations exceeding 100 millions, but these were associations of divergent•peoples; there has never been one single people on this scale before. We want a new term for this new thing. We call the United States a country, just as we call France or Holland a country. But really the two things are as different as an automobile and a one-horse shay. They are the creations of different periods and different conditions; they are going to work at a different pace and in an entirely different way. If you propose—as I gather some of the League of Nations people propose—to push the Peace of the World along on a combination of these two sorts of vehicle, I venture to think the Peace of the World will be subjected to some very considerable strains.

Let me now make a brief comparison between the American and the European situation in relation to these vital matters, locomotion and the general means of communicating. I said just now that the United States of America owe most to the revolution in locomotion and have felt it least. Europe on the other hand owes least to the revolution in locomotion and has felt it most. The revolution in locomotion found the United States of America a fringe of population on the sea margins of a great rich virgin empty country into which it desired to expand, and into which it was free to expand. The steamboat and railway seemed to come as a natural part of that expansion. They came as unqualified blessings. But into Western Europe they came as a frightful nuisance.

The States of Europe, excepting Russia, were already a settled, established and balanced system. They were living in final and conclusive boundaries with no further possibility of peaceful expansion. Every extension of a European state involved a war; it was only possible through war. And while the limits to the United States have been set by the steamship and the railroad, the limits to the European sovereign states were drawn at a much earlier time. They were drawn by the horse, and particularly the coach-horse travelling along the high road. If you will examine a series of political maps of Europe for the last two thousand years, you will see that there has evidently been a definite limit to the size of sovereign states through all that time, due to the impossibility of keeping them together because of the difficulty of intercommunication if they grew bigger. And this was in spite of the fact that there were two great unifying ideas present in men's minds in Europe through-

out that period, namely, the unifying idea of the
Roman Empire, and the unifying idea of Christendom. Both these ideas tended to make Europe
one, but the difficulties of communication defeated
that tendency. It is quite interesting to watch the
adventures of what is called first the Roman Empire and afterwards the Holy Roman Empire, in a
series of historical maps. It keeps expanding and
then dropping to pieces again. It is like the efforts
of someone who is trying to pack up a parcel which
is much took big, in wet blotting paper. The cohesion was inadequate. And so it was that the eighteenth century found Europe still divided up into
what I may perhaps call these high-road and
coach-horse states, each with a highly developed
foreign policy, each with an intense sense of national difference and each with intense traditional
antagonisms.

Then came this revolution in the means of locomotion, which has increased the normal range of
human activity at least ten times. The effect of
that in America was opportunity; the effect of it
in Europe was congestion. It is as if some rather
careless worker of miracles had decided suddenly
to make giants of a score of ordinary men, and
chose the moment for the miracle when they were
all with one exception strap-hanging in a street
car. The United States was that fortunate exception.

Now this is what modern civilization has come
up against, and it is the essential riddle of the
modern sphinx which must be solved if we are to

live. All the European boundaries of to-day are impossibly small for modern conditions. And they are sustained by an intensity of ancient tradition and patriotic passion. . . . That is where we stand.

The citizens of the United States of America are not without their experience in this matter. The crisis of the national history of the American community, the war between Union and Secession, was essentially a crisis between the great state of the new age and the local feeling of an earlier period. But Union triumphed. Americans live now in a generation that has almost forgotten that there once seemed a possibility that the map of North America might be broken up at last into as many communities as the map of Europe. Except by foreign travel, the present generation of Americans can have no idea of the net of vexations and limitations in which Europeans are living at the present time because of their political disunion.

Let me take a small but quite significant set of differences, the inconveniences of travel upon a journey of a little over a thousand miles. They are in themselves petty inconveniences, but they will serve to illustrate the net that is making free civilized life in Europe more and more impossible.

Take first the American case. An American wants to travel from New York to St. Louis. He looks up the next train, packs his bag, gets aboard a sleeper and turns out at St. Louis next day ready for business.

Take now the European parallel. A European

wants to travel from London to Warsaw. Now
that is a shorter distance by fifty or sixty miles
than the distance from New York to St. Louis.
Will *he* pack his bag, get aboard a train and go
there? He will not. He will have to get a passport, and getting a passport involves all sorts of
tiresome little errands. One has to go to a photog-
rapher, for example, to get photographs to stick
on the passport. The good European has then to
take his passport to the French representative in
London for a French visa, or, if he is going
through Belgium, for a Belgian visa. After that
he must get a German visa. Then he must go
round to the Czecho-Slovak office for a Czecho-
Slovak visa. Finally will·come the Polish visa.

Each of these endorsements necessitates something vexatious, personal attendance, photogra-
phy, stamps, rubber stamps, mysterious signa-
tures and the like, and always the payment of fees.
Also they necessitate delays. The other day I had
occasion to go to Moscow, and I learnt that it
takes three weeks to get a visa for Finland and
three weeks to get a visa for Esthonia. You see
you can't travel about Europe at all without weeks
and weeks of preparation. The preparations for
a little journey to Russia the other day took three
whole days out of my life, cost me several pounds
in stamps and fees, and five in bribery.

Ultimately, however, the good European is free
to start. Arriving at the French frontier in an
hour or so, he will be held up for a long customs'
examination. Also he will need to change some

of his money into francs. His English money will
be no good in France. The exchange in Europe
is always fluctuating, and he will be cheated on the
exchange. All European countries, including my
own, cheat travellers on the exchange—that is
apparently what the exchange is for.

He will then travel for a few hours to the German frontier. There he will be bundled out again.
The French will investigate him closely to see that
he is not carrying gold or large sums of money
out of France. Then he will be handed over to the
Germans. He will go through the same business
with the customs and the same business with the
money. His French money is no further use to
him and he must get German. A few more hours
and he will arrive on the frontier of Bohemia.
Same search for gold. Then customs' examination
and change of money again. A few hours more
and he will be in Poland. Search for gold, customs, fresh money.

As most of these countries are pursuing different railway policies, he will probably have to
change trains and rebook his luggage three or four
times. The trains may be ingeniously contrived
not to connect so as to force him to take some
longer route politically favoured by one of the intervening states. He will be lucky if he gets to
Warsaw in four days.

Arrived in Warsaw, he will probably need a
permit to stay there, and he will certainly need no
end of permits to leave.

Now here is a fuss over a fiddling little journey

of 1,100 miles. Is it any wonder that the bookings from London to Warsaw are infinitesimal in comparison with the bookings from New York to St. Louis? But what I have noted here are only the normal inconveniences of the traveller. They are by no means the most serious inconveniences.

The same obstructions that hamper the free movement of a traveller, hamper the movement of foodstuffs and all sorts of merchandise in a much greater degree. Everywhere in Europe trade is being throttled by tariffs and crippled by the St. Vitus' dance of the exchanges. Each of these European sovereign states turns out paper money at its own sweet will. Last summer I went to Prague and exchanged pounds for kroners. They ought to have been 25 to the pound. On Monday they were 180 to the pound: on Friday 169. They jump about between 220 and 150, and everybody is inconvenienced except the bankers and money changers. And this uncertain exchange diverts considerable amounts of money that should be stimulating business enterprise into a barren and mischievous gambling with the circulation.

Between each one of these compressed European countries the movement of food or labour is still more blocked and impeded. And in addition to these nuisances of national tariffs and independent national coinages at every few score miles, Europe is extraordinarily crippled by its want of any central authority to manage the most elementary collective interests; the control of vice, for example; the handling of infectious diseases; the suppression of international criminals.

Europe is now confronted by a new problem— the problem of air transport. So far as I can see, air transport is going to be strangled in Europe by international difficulties. One can fly comfortably and safely from London to Paris in two or three hours. But the passport preliminaries will take days beforehand.

The other day I wanted to get quickly to Reval in Esthonia from England and back again. The distance is about the same as from Boston to Minneapolis, and it could be done comfortably in 10 or 12 hours' flying. I proposed to the Handley, Page Company that they should arrange this for me. They explained that they had no power to fly beyond Amsterdam in Holland; thence it might be possible to get a German plane to Hamburg, and thence again a Danish plane to Copenhagen— leaving about 500 miles which were too complicated politically to fly. Each stoppage would involve passport and other difficulties. In the end it took me five days to get to Reval and seven days to get back. In Europe, with its present frontiers, flying is not worth having. It can never be worth having—it can never be worked successfully—until it is worked as at least a pan-European affair.

All these are the normal inconveniences of the national divisions of Europe in peace time. By themselves they are strangling all hope of economic recovery. For Europe is *not* getting on to its feet economically. Only a united effort can effect that. But along each of the ridiculously restricted frontiers into which the European countries are packed, lies also the possibility of war. National independence means the right to declare war. And so each of these packed and strangulated European countries is obliged, by its blessed independence, to maintain as big an army and as big a military equipment as its bankrupt condition —for we are all bankrupt—permits.

Since the end of the great war, nothing has been done of any real value to ensure any European country against the threat of war, and nothing will be done, and nothing can be done to lift that threat, so long as the idea of national independence overrides all other considerations.

And again, it is a little difficult for a mind accustomed to American conditions, to realize what modern war will mean in Europe.

Not one of these sovereign European states I have named between London and Warsaw is any larger than the one single American state of Texas, and not one has a capital that cannot be effectively bombed by aeroplane raiders from its frontier within five or six hours of a declaration of war. We can fly from London to Paris in two or three hours. And the aerial bombs of to-day, I can assure you, will make the biggest bombs of 1918 seem like little crackers. Over all these European countries broods this immediate threat of a warfare that will strain and torment the nerves of every living man, woman or child in the countries affected. Nothing of the sort can approach the

American citizen except after a long warning. The worst war that could happen to any North American country would merely touch its coasts.

Now I have dwelt on these differences between America and Europe because they involve an absolute difference in outlook towards world peace projects, towards leagues of nations, world states and the like, between the American and the European.

The American lives in a political unity on the big modern scale. He can go on comfortably for a hundred years yet before he begins to feel tight in his political skin, and before he begins to feel the threat of immediate warfare close to his domestic life. He believes by experience in peace, but he feels under no passionate urgency to organize it. So far as he himself is concerned, he has got peace organized for a good long time ahead. I doubt if it would make any very serious difference for some time in the ordinary daily life of Kansas City, let us say, if all Europe were reduced to a desert in the next five years.

But on the other hand, the intelligent European is up against the unity of Europe problem night and day. Europe cannot go on. European civilization cannot go on, unless that net of boundaries which strangles her is dissolved away. The difficulties created by language differences, by bitter national traditions, by bad political habits and the like, are no doubt stupendous. But stupendous though they are, they have to be faced. Unless they are overcome, and overcome in a very few

years, Europe—entangled in this net of boundaries, and under a perpetual fear of war, will, I
am convinced, follow Russia and slide down beyond any hope of recovery into a process of social
dissolution as profound and disastrous as that
which closed the career of the Western Roman
Empire.

The American intelligence and the European
intelligence approach this question of a world
peace, therefore, from an entirely different angle
and in an entirely different spirit. To the American in the blessed ease of his great unbroken territory, it seems a matter simply of making his
own ample securities world-wide by treaties of
arbitration and such-like simple agreements. And
my impression is that he thinks of Europeans as
living under precisely similar conditions.

Nothing of that sort will meet the problem of
the old world. The European situation is altogether more intense and tragic than the American.
Europe needs not treaties but a profound change
in its political ideas and habits. Europe is saturated with narrow patriotism like a body saturated
by some evil inherited disease. She is haunted by
narrow ambitions and ancient animosities.

It is because of this profound difference of situation and outlook that I am convinced of the impossibility of any common political co-operation
to organize a world peace between America and
Europe at the present time.

The American type of state and the European
type of state are different things, incapable of an

effectual alliance; the steam tractor and the ox cannot plough this furrow together. American thought, American individuals, may no doubt play a very great part in the task of reconstruction that lies before Europe, but not the American federal government as a sovereign state among equal states.

The United States constitute a state on a different scale and level from any old world state. Patriotism and the national idea in America is a different thing and a bigger scale thing than the patriotism and national idea in any old world state.

Any League of Nations aiming at stability now, would necessarily be a league seeking to stereotype existing boundaries and existing national ideas. Now these boundaries and these ideas are just what have to be got rid of at any cost. Before Europe can get on to a level and on to equal terms with the United States, the European communities have to go through a process that America went through—under much easier conditions—a century and a half ago. They have to repeat, on a much greater scale and against profounder prejudices, the feat of understanding and readjustment that was accomplished by the American people between 1781 and 1788.

As you will all remember, these States after they had decided upon Independence, framed certain Articles of Confederation; they were articles of confederation between thirteen nations, between the people of Massachusetts, the people of Vir-

ginia, the people of Georgia, and so forth—thirteen distinct and separate sovereign peoples.
They made a Union so lax and feeble that it could
neither keep order at home nor maintain respect
abroad. Then they produced another constitution. They swept aside all that talk about the people of Massachusetts, the people of Virginia, and
the rest of their thirteen nations. They based their
union on a wider idea: the people of the United
States.

Now Europe, if it is not to sink down to anar-
chy, has to do a parallel thing. If Europe is to
be saved from ultimate disaster, Europe has to
stop thinking in terms of the people of France,
the people of England, the people of Germany,
the French, the British, the Germans, and so forth.
Europe has to think at least of the people of
Europe, if not of the civilized people of the world.
If we Europeans cannot bring our minds to that,
there is no hope for us. Only by thinking of all
peoples can any people be saved in Europe. Fresh
wars will destroy the social fabric of Europe, and
Europe will perish as nations, fighting.

There are many people who think that there is at
least one political system in the old world which,
like the United States, is large enough and world-
wide enough to go on by itself under modern conditions for some considerable time. They think
that the British Empire can, as it were, stand out
of the rest of the Old World as a self-sufficient
system. They think that it can stand out freely
as the United States can stand out, and that these

two English-speaking powers have merely to agree together to dominate and keep the peace of the world.

Let me give a little attention to this idea. It is I believe a wrong idea, and one that may be véry disastrous to our common English-speaking culture if it is too fondly cherished.

There can be no denying that the British Imperial system is a system different in its nature and size from a typical European state, from a state of the horse and road scale, like France, let us say, or Germany. And equally it is with the United States a new growth. The present British Empire is indeed a newer growth than the United States. But while the United States constitute a homogeneous system and grow more homogeneous, the British Empire is heterogeneous and shows little or no assimilative power. And while the United States are all gathered together and are still very remote from any serious antagonist, the British Empire is scattered all over the world, entangled with and stressed against a multitude of possible antagonists.

I have been arguing that the size and manageability of all political states is finally a matter of transport and communications. They grow to a limit strictly determined by these considerations. Beyond that limit they are unstable. Let us now apply these ideas to the British Empire.

I have shown that the great system of the United States is the creation of the river steamboat and the railway. Quite as much so is the present British Empire the creation of the ocean-going steamship—protected by a great navy.

The British Empire is a modern ocean state just as the United States is a modern continental state. The political and economic cohesion of the British Empire rests upon this one thing, upon the steamship remaining the dominant and secure means of world transport in the future. If the British Empire is to remain sovereign and secure and independent of the approval and co-operation of other states, it is necessary that steamship transport (ocean transport) should remain dominant in peace and invulnerable in war.

Well, that brings us face to face with two comparatively new facts that throw a shadow upon both that predominance and upon that invulnerability. One is air transport; the other the submarine. The possibilities of the ocean-going submarine I will not enlarge upon now. They will be familiar to everyone who followed the later phases of the great war.

It must be clear that sea power is no longer the simple and decisive thing it was before the coming of the submarine. The sea ways can no longer be taken and possessed completely. To no other power, except Japan, is this so grave a consideration as it is to Britain.

And if we turn to the possibilities of air-transport in the future we are forced towards the same conclusion, that the security of the British Empire must rest in the future not on its strength in warfare, but on its keeping the peace within and without its boundaries.

I was a member of the British Civil Air Transport Committee, and we went with care and thoroughness into the possibilities and probabilities of the air. My work on that committee convinced me that in the near future the air may be the chief if not the only highway for long-distance mails, for long-distance passenger traffic, and for the carriage of most valuable and compact commodities. The ocean ways are likely to be only the ways for slow travel and for staple and bulky trade.

And my studies on that committee did much to confirm my opinion that in quite a brief time the chief line of military attack will be neither by sea nor land but through the air. Moreover, it was borne in upon me that the chief air routes of the world will lie over the great plains of the world, that they will cross wide stretches of sea or mountainous country only very reluctantly.

Now think of how the British Empire lies with relation to the great sea and land masses of the world. There has been talk in Great Britain of what people have called "all-red air routes," that is to say, all-British air routes. There are no all-red air routes. You cannot get out of Britain to any other parts of the Empire, unless perhaps it is Canada, without crossing foreign territory. That is a fact that British people have to face and digest, and the sooner they grasp it the better for them. Britain cannot use air ways even to develop her commerce in peace time without the consent and co-operation of a large number of her intervening neighbours. If she embarks single-handed on any considerable war she will find both her air and her sea communications almost completely cut.

And so the British Empire, in spite of its size and its modernity, is not much better off now in the way of standing alone than the other European countries. It is no exception to our generalization that (apart from all other questions) the scale and form of the European states are out of harmony with contemporary and developing transport conditions, and that all these powers are, if only on this account, under one urgent necessity to sink those ideas of complete independence that have hitherto dominated them. It is a life and death necessity. If they cannot obey it they will all be destroyed.

III

In my opening argument I have shown the connection between the present intense political troubles of the world and more particularly of Europe, and the advance in mechanical knowledge during the past hundred and fifty years. I have shown that without a very drastic readjustment of political ideas and habits, there opens before Europe and the world generally, a sure prospect of degenerative conflicts; that without such a readjustment, our civilization has passed its zenith and must continue the process of collapse that has been in progress since August, 1914.

Now this readjustment means an immediate conflict with existing patriotism. We have embarked here upon a discussion in which emotion and passion seem quite unavoidable, the discussion of nationality. At the very outset we bump violently against patriotism as any European understands that word. And it is, I hold, impossible not to bump against European patriotisms. We cannot temporize with patriotism, as one finds it in Europe, and get on towards a common human welfare. The two things are flatly opposed. One or the other must be sacrificed. The political and social

70

muddle of Europe at the present time is very largely due to the attempt to compromise between patriotism and the common good of Europe.

Do we want to get rid of patriotism altogether?

I do not think we want to get rid of patriotism, and I do not think we could, even if we wanted to do so. It seems to be necessary to his moral life, that a man should feel himself part of a community, belonging to it, and it belonging to him. And that this community should be a single and lovable reality, inspired by a common idea, with a common fashion and aim.

But a point I have been trying to bring out throughout all this argument so far is this—that when a European goes to the United States of America he finds a new sort of state, materially bigger and materially less encumbered than any European state. And he also finds an intensely patriotic people whose patriotism isn't really the equivalent of a European patriotism. It is historically and practically a synthesis of European patriotisms. It is numerically bigger. It is geographically ten times as big. That is very important indeed from the point of view of this discussion. And it is synthetic; it is a thing made out of something smaller. People, I believe, talk of 100 per cent. Americans. There is no 100 per cent. American except the Red Indian. There isn't a white man in the United States from whose blood a large factor of European patriotism hasn't been washed out to make way for his American patriotism.

Upon this fact of American patriotism, as a larger different thing than European patriotism, I build. The thing can be done. If it can be done in the Europeans and their descendants who have come to America, it can conceivably be done in the Europeans who abide in Europe. And how can we set about doing it?

America, the silent, comprehensive continent of America, did the thing by taking all the various nationalities who have made up her population and obliging them to live together.

Unhappily we cannot take the rest of our European nations now and put them on to a great virgin continent to learn a wider political wisdom. There are no more virgin continents. Europe must stay where she is. . . .

Now I am told it sometimes helps scientific men to clear up their ideas about a process by imagining that process reversed and so getting a view of it from a different direction. Let us then, for a few moments, instead of talking of the expansion and synthesis of patriotism in Europe, imagine a development of narrow patriotism in America and consider how that case could be dealt with.

Suppose, for instance, there was a serious outbreak of local patriotism in Kentucky. Suppose you found the people of Kentucky starting a flag of their own and objecting to what they would probably call the "vague internationalism" of the stars and stripes. Suppose you found them wanting to set up tariff barriers to the trade of the states round about them. Suppose you found they

were preparing to annex considerable parts of the
State of Virginia by force, in order to secure a
proper strategic frontier among the mountains to
the east, and that they were also talking darkly of
their need for an outlet to the sea of their very
own.

What would an American citizen think of such
an outbreak? He would probably think that Kentucky had gone mad. But this, which seems such
fantastic behaviour when we imagine it occurring
in Kentucky, is exactly what is happening in Europe in the case of little states that are hardly
any larger than Kentucky. They have always
been so. They have not gone mad; if this sort
of thing is madness then they were born mad.
And they have never been cured. A state of affairs that is regarded in Europe as normal would
be regarded in the United States as a grave case
of local mental trouble.

And what would the American community probably do in such a case? It would probably begin
by inquiring where Kentucky had got these
strange ideas. They would look for sources of
infection. Somebody must have been preaching
there or writing in the newspapers or teaching
mischief in the school. And I suppose the people
of the United States would set themselves very
earnestly to see that sounder sense was talked and
taught to the people of Kentucky about these
things.

Now that is precisely what has to be done in
the parallel European case. Everywhere in Eu-

rope there goes on in the national schools, in the patriotic churches, in the national presses, in the highly nationalized literatures, a unity-destroying propaganda of patriotism. The schools of all the European countries at the present time with scarcely an exception, teach the most rancid patriotism; they are centres of an abominable political infection. The children of Europe grow up with an intensity of national egotism that makes them, for all practical international purposes, insane. They are not born with it, but they are infected with it as soon as they can read and write. The British learn nothing but the glories of Britain and the British Empire; the French are, if possible, still more insanely concentrated on France; the Germans are just recovering from the bitter consequences of forty years of intensive nationalist education. And so on. Every country in Europe is its own *Sinn Fein,* cultivating that ugly and silly obsession of "ourselves alone." "Ourselves alone" is the sure guide to conflict and disaster, to want, misery, violence, degradation and death for our children and our children's children —until our race is dead.

The first task before us in Europe is, at any cost, to release our children from this nationalist obsession, to teach the mass of European people a little truthful history in which each one will see the past and future of his own country in their proper proportions, and a little truthful ethnology in which each country will get over the delusion that its people are a distinct and individual race.

The history teaching in the schools of Europe is at the very core of this business.

But that is only, so to speak, the point of application of great complex influences, the influences that mould us in childhood, the teachings of literature, of the various religious bodies, and the daily reiteration of the press. Before Europe can get on, there has to be a colossal turnover of these moral and intellectual forces in the direction of creating an international mind. If that can be effected then there is hope for Europe and the Old World. If it cannot be effected, then certainly Europe will go down—with its flags nailed to its masts. We are on a sinking ship that only one thing can save. We have to oust these European patriotisms by some greater idea or perish.

What is this greater idea to be?

Now I submit that this greater idea had best be the idea of the World State of All Mankind.

I will admit that so far I have made a case only for teaching the idea of a United States of Europe in Europe. I have concentrated our attention upon that region of maximum congestion and conflict. But as a matter of fact there are no real and effective barriers and boundaries in the Old World between Europe and Asia and Africa. The ordinary Russian talks of "Europe" as one who is outside it. The European political systems flow over and have always overflowed into the greater areas to the east and south. Remember the early empires of Macedonia and Rome. See how the Russian language runs to the Pacific, and

how Islam radiates into all three continents. I
will not elaborate this case.

When you bear such things in mind, I think
you will agree with me that if we are to talk of
a United States of Europe, it is just as easy and
practicable to talk of a United States of the Old
World. And are we to stop at a United States
of the Old World?

No doubt the most evident synthetic forces in
America at the present time point towards some
sort of pan-American unification. That is the
nearest thing. That may come first.

But are we to contemplate a sort of dual world
—the New World against the Old?

I do not think that would be any very perma-
nent or satisfactory stopping-place. Why make
two bites at a planet? If we work for unity on
the large scale we are contemplating, we may as
well work for world unity.

Not only in distance but in a score of other
matters are London and Rome nearer to New
York than is Patagonia, and San Francisco is
always likely to be more interesting to Japan than
Paris or Madrid. I cannot see any reason for
supposing that the mechanical drawing together
of the peoples of the world into one economic
and political unity is likely to cease—unless our
civilization ceases. I see no signs that our present
facilities for transport and communication are the
ultimate possible facilities. Once we break away
from current nationalist limitations in our political ideas, then there is no reason and no advantage

in contemplating any halfway house to a complete human unity.

Now after what I have been saying it is very easy to explain why I would have this idea of human unity put before people's minds in the form of a World State and not of a League of Nations.

Let me first admit the extraordinary educational value of the League of Nations propaganda, and of the attempt that has been made to create a League of Nations. It has brought before the general intelligence of the world the proposition of a world law and a world unity that could not perhaps have been broached in any other way.

But is it a league of nations that is wanted?

I submit to you that the word "nations" is just the word that should have been avoided—that it admits and tends to stereotype just those conceptions of division and difference that we must at any cost minimize and obliterate if our species is to continue. And the phrase has a thin and legal and litigious flavour. What loyalty and what devotion can we expect this multiple association to command? It has no unity—no personality. It is like asking a man to love the average member of a woman's club instead of loving his wife.

For the idea of Man, for human unity, for our common blood, for the one order of the world, I can imagine men living and dying, but not for a miscellaneous assembly that will not mix—even in its name. It has no central idea, no heart to it, this League of Nations formula. It is weak and compromising just where it should be strong

—in defining its antagonism to separate national sovereignty. For that is what it aims at, if it means business. If it means business it means at least a super-state overriding the autonomy of existing states, and if it does not mean business then we have no use for it whatever.

It may seem a much greater undertaking to attack nationality and nationalism instead of patching up a compromise with these things, but along the line of independent nationality lies no hope of unity and peace and continuing progress for mankind. We cannot suffer these old concentrations of loyalty because we want that very loyalty which now concentrates upon them to cement and sustain the peace of all the world. Just as in the past provincial patriotisms have given place to national patriotisms, so now we need to oust these still too narrow devotions by a new unity and a new reigning idea, the idea of one state and one flag in all the earth.

The idea of the World States stands to the idea of the League of Nations much as the idea of the one God of Earth and Heaven stands to a Divine Committee composed of Wodin and Baal and Jupiter and Amnon Ra and Mumbo Jumbo and all the other national and tribal gods. There is no compromise possible in the one matter as in the other. There is no way round. The task before mankind is to substitute the one common idea of an overriding world commonweal for the multitudinous ideas of little commonweals that prevail everywhere to-day. We have already glanced at the near and current consequences of our failure to bring about that substitution.

Now this is an immense proposal. Is it a preposterous one? Let us not shirk the tremendous scale upon which the foundations of a world-state of all mankind must be laid. But remember however great that task before us may seem, however near it may come to the impossible, nevertheless, in the establishment of one world rule and one world law lies the only hope of escape from an increasing tangle of wars, from social over-strain, and at last a social dissolution so complete as to end for ever the tale of mankind as we understand mankind.

Personally I am appalled by the destruction already done in the world in the past seven years. I doubt if any untravelled American can realize how much of Europe is already broken up. I do not think many people realize how swiftly Europe is still sinking, how urgent it is to get European affairs put back upon a basis of the common good if civilization is to be saved.

And now, as to the immensity of this project of substituting loyalty to a world commonweal for loyalty to a single egotistical belligerent nation. It is a project to invade hundreds of millions of minds, to attack certain ideas established in those minds and either to efface those ideas altogether or to supplement and correct them profoundly by this new idea of a human commonweal. We have to get not only into the at present intensely patriotic minds of Frenchmen, Germans, English,

Irish and Japanese, but into the remote and difficult minds of Arabs and Indians and into the minds of the countless millions of China. Is there any precedent to justify us in hoping that such a change in world ideas is possible?

I think there is. I would suggest that the general tendency of thought about these things to-day is altogether too sceptical of what teaching and propaganda can do in these matters. In the past there have been very great changes in human thought. I need scarcely remind you of the spread of Christianity in Western Europe. In a few centuries the whole of Western Europe was changed from the wild confusion of warring tribes that succeeded the breakdown of the Roman Empire, into the unity of Christendom, into a community with such an idea of unity that it could be roused from end to end by the common idea of the Crusades.

Still more remarkable was the swift transformation in less than a century of all the nations and peoples to the south and west of the Mediterranean, from Spain to Central Asia, into the unity of Islam, a unity which has lasted to this day. In both these cases, what I may call the mental turnover was immense.

I think if you will consider the spread of these very complex and difficult religions, and compare the means at the disposal of their promoters with the means at the disposal of intelligent people to-day, you will find many reasons for believing that a recasting of people's ideas into the framework of a universal state is by no means an impossible project.

Those great teachings of the past were spread largely by word of mouth. Their teachers had to travel slowly and dangerously. People were gathered together to hear with great difficulty, except in a few crowded towns. Books could be used only sparingly. Few people could read, fewer still could translate, and MSS. were copied with extreme slowness upon parchment. There was no printing, no paper, no post. And except for a very few people there were no schools. Both Christendom and Islam had to create their common schools in order to preserve even a minimum of their doctrine intact from generation to generation. All this was done in the teeth of much bitter opposition and persecution.

Now to-day we have means of putting ideas and arguments swiftly and effectively before people all over the world at the same time, such as no one could have dreamt of a hundred years ago. We have not only books and papers, but in the cinema we have a means of rapid, vivid presentation still hardly used. We have schools nearly everywhere. And here in the need for an overruling world state, and the idea of world service replacing combative patriotism, we have an urgent, a commanding human need. We have an invincible case for this world state and an unanswerable objection to the nationalisms and patriotisms that would oppose it.

Is it not almost inevitable that some of us should

get together and begin a propaganda upon modern lines of this organized world peace, without which our race must perish? The world perishes for the want of a common political idea. It is still quite possible to give the world this common political idea, the idea of a federal world state. We cannot help but set about doing it.

So I put it to you that the most important work before men and women to-day is the preaching and teaching, the elaboration and then at last the realization of this Project of the World State. We have to create a vision of it, to make it seem first a possibility and then an approaching reality. This is a task that demands the work and thought of thousands of minds. We have to spread the idea of a Federal World State, as an approaching reality, throughout the world. We can do this nowadays through a hundred various channels. We can do it through the press, through all sorts of literary expression, in our schools, colleges, and universities, through political mouthpieces, by special organizations, and last, but not least, through the teaching of the churches. For remember that all the great religions of the world are in theory universalist; they may tolerate the divisions of men but they cannot sanction them. We propose no religious revolution, but at most a religious revival. We can spread ideas and suggestions now with a hundred times the utmost rapidity of a century ago.

This movement need not at once intervene in politics. It is a prospective movement, and its

special concern will be with young and still growing minds. But as it spreads it will inevitably
change politics. The nations, states, and king-
doms of to-day, which fight and scheme against
each other as though they had to go on fighting
and scheming for ever, will become more and more
openly and manifestly merely guardian governments, governments playing a waiting part in the
world, while the world state comes of age. For
this World State, for which the world is waiting,
must necessarily be a fusion of all governments,
and heir to all the empires.

So far I have been occupied by establishing a
case for the World State. It has been, I fear,
rather an abstract discussion. I have kept closely
to the bare hard logic of the present human situation.

But now let me attempt very briefly, in the
barest outline, some concrete realization of what
a World State would mean. Let us try and conceive for ourselves the form a World State would
take. I do not care to leave this discussion with
nothing to it but a phrase which is really hardly
more than a negative phrase until we put some
body to it. As it stands World State means simply
a politically undivided world. Let us try and
carry that over to the idea of a unified organized
state throughout the world.

Let us try to imagine what a World Government would be like. I find that when one speaks
of a World State people think at once of some
existing government and magnify it to world pro-

portions. They ask, for example, where will the
World Congress meet; and how will you elect your
World President? Won't your World President,
they say, be rather a tremendous personage? How
are we to choose him? Or will there be a World
King? These are very natural questions, at the
first onset. But are they sound questions?
May they not be a little affected by false analogies? The governing of the whole of the world
may turn out to be *not* a magnified version of
governing a part of the world, but a different sort
of job altogether. These analogies that people
draw so readily from national states may not
really work in a World State.

And first with regard to this question of a
king or president. Let us ask whether it is prob-
able that the World State will have any single
personal head at all?

Is the World State likely to be a monarchy—
either an elective short term limited monarchy
such as is the United States, or an inherited
limited monarchy like the British Empire?

Many people will say, you *must* have a head of
the state. But *must* you? Is not this idea a
legacy from the days when states were small communities needing a leader in war and diplomacy?

In the World State we must remember there
will be no war—and no diplomacy as such.

I would even question whether in such a great
modern state as the U.S.A. the idea and the
functions of the president may not be made too
important. Indeed I believe that question has

been asked by many people in the States lately, and has been answered in the affirmative.

The broad lines of the United States Constitution were drawn in a period of almost universal monarchy. American affairs were overshadowed by the personality of George Washington, and as you know, monarchist ideas were so rife that there was a project, during the years of doubt and division that followed the War of Independence, for importing a German King, a Prussian Prince, in imitation of the British Monarchy. But if the United States were beginning again to-day on its present scale, would it put so much power and importance upon a single individual as it put upon George Washington and his successors in the White House? I doubt it very much.

There may be a limit, I suggest, to the size and complexity of a community that can be directed by a single personal head. Perhaps that limit may have been passed by both the United States and by the British Empire at the present time. It may be possible for one person to be leader and to have an effect of directing personality in a community of millions or even of tens of millions. But is it possible for one small short-lived individual to get over and affect and make any sort of contact with hundreds of millions in thousands of towns and cities?

Recently we have watched with admiration and sympathy the heroic efforts of the Prince of Wales to shake hands with and get his smile well home into the hearts of the entire population of the

British Empire of which he is destined to become the "golden link." After tremendous exertions a very large amount of the ground still remains to be covered.

I will confess I cannot see any single individual human head in my vision of the World State.

The linking reality of the World State is much more likely to be not an individual but an idea—such an idea as that of a human commonweal under the God of all mankind.

If at any time, for any purpose, some one individual had to step out and act for the World State as a whole, then I suppose the senior judges of the Supreme Court, or the Speaker of the Council, or the head of the Associated Scientific Societies, or some such person, could step out and do what had to be done.

But if there is to be no single head person, there must be at least some sort of assembly or council. That seems to be necessary. But will it be a gathering at all like Congress or the British Parliament, with a Government side and an opposition ruled by party traditions and party ideas?

There again, I think we may be too easily misled by existing but temporary conditions. I do not think it is necessary to assume that the council of the World State will be an assembly of party politicians. I believe it will be possible to have it a real gathering of representatives, a fair sample of the thought and will of mankind at large, and to avoid a party development by a more scientific method of voting than the barbaric devices used for electing representatives to Congress or the British Parliament, devices that play directly into the hands of the party organizer who trades upon the defects of political method.

Will this council be directly elected? That, I think, may be found to be essential. And upon a very broad franchise. Because, *firstly,* it is before all things important that every adult in the world should feel a direct and personal contact between himself and the World State, and that he is an assenting and participating citizen of the world; and *secondly,* because if your Council is appointed by any intermediate body, all sorts of local and national considerations, essential in the business of the subordinate body, will get in the way of a simple and direct regard for the world commonweal.

And as to this council: Will it have great debates and wonderful scenes and crises and so forth—the sort of thing that looks well in a large historical painting? There again we may be easily misled by analogy. One consideration that bars the way to anything of that sort is that its members will have no common language which they will be all able to speak with the facility necessary for eloquence. Eloquence is far more adapted to the conditions of a Red Indian pow-wow than to the ordering of large and complicated affairs. The World Council may be a very taciturn assembly. It may even meet infrequently. Its members may communicate their views largely by *notes* which may have to be very clear and explicit, because they will have to stand translation, and short—to escape neglect.

And what will be the chief organs and organizations and works and methods with which this Council of the World State will be concerned?

There will be a Supreme Court determining *not* International Law, but World Law. There will be a growing Code of World Law.

There will be a world currency.

There will be a ministry of posts, transport and communications generally.

There will be a ministry of trade in staple products and for the conservation and development of the natural resources of the earth.

There will be a ministry of social and labour conditions.

There will be a ministry of world health.

There will be a ministry, the most important ministry of all, watching and supplementing national educational work and taking up the care and stimulation of backward communities.

And instead of a War Office and Naval and Military departments, there will be a *Peace Ministry* studying the belligerent possibilities of every new invention, watching for armed disturbances everywhere, and having complete control of every armed force that remains in the world. All these world ministries will be working in co-operation with local authorities who will apply world-wide general principles to local conditions.

These items probably comprehend everything

that the government of a World State would have
to do. Much of its activity would be merely the
co-ordination and adjustment of activities already
very thoroughly discussed and prepared for it by
local and national discussions. I think it will be
a mistake for us to assume that the work of a
world government will be vaster and more complex
than that of such governments as those of the
United States or the British Empire. In many
respects it will have an enormously simplified task.
There will be no foreign enemy, no foreign com-
petition, no tariffs, so far as it is concerned, or
tariff wars. It will be keeping order; it will not
be carrying on a contest. There will be no necessity for secrecy; it will not be necessary to have
a Cabinet plotting and planning behind closed
doors; there will be no general policy except a
steady attention to the common welfare. Even
the primary origin of a World Council must necessarily be different from that of any national government. Every existing government owes its
beginnings to force and is in its fundamental
nature militant. It is an offensive-defensive
organ. This fact saturates our legal and social
tradition more than one realizes at first. There is,
about civil law everywhere, a faint flavour of a
relaxed state of siege. But a world government
will arise out of different motives and realize a
different ideal. It will be primarily an organ for
keeping the peace.

And now perhaps we may look at this project
of a World State mirrored in the circumstances of

the life of one individual citizen. Let us consider very briefly the life of an ordinary young man living in a World State and consider how it would differ from a commonplace life to-day.

He will have been born in some one of the United States of the World—in New York or California or Ontario or New Zealand or Portugal or France or Bengal or Shan-si; but wherever his lot may fall, the first history he will learn will be the wonderful history of mankind, from its nearly animal beginnings, a few score thousand years ago, with no tools, but implements of chipped stone and hacked wood, up to the power and knowledge of our own time. His education will trace for him the beginnings of speech, of writing, of cultivation and settlement.

He will learn of the peoples and nations of the past, and how each one has brought its peculiar gifts and its distinctive contribution to the accumulating inheritance of our race.

He will know, perhaps, less of wars, battles, conquests, massacres, kings and the like unpleasant invasions of human dignity and welfare, and he will know more of explorers, discoverers and stout outspoken men than our contemporary citizen.

While he is still a little boy, he will have the great outlines of the human adventure brought home to his mind by all sorts of vivid methods of presentation, such as the poor poverty-struck schools of our own time cannot dream of employing.

And on this broad foundation he will build up his knowledge of his own particular state and nation and people, learning not tales of ancient grievances and triumphs and revenges, but what his particular race and countryside have given and what it gives and may be expected to give to the common welfare of the world. On such foundations his social consciousness will be built.

He will learn an outline of all that mankind knows and of the fascinating realms of half knowledge in which man is still struggling to know. His curiosity and his imagination will be roused and developed.

He will probably be educated continuously at least until he is eighteen or nineteen, and perhaps until he is two or three and twenty. For a world that wastes none of its resources upon armaments or soldiering, and which produces whatever it wants in the regions best adapted to that production, and delivers them to the consumer by the directest route, will be rich enough not only to spare the first quarter of everybody's life for education entirely, but to keep on with some education throughout the whole lifetime.

Of course the school to which our young citizen of the world will go will be very different from the rough and tumble schools of to-day, understaffed with underpaid assistants, and having bare walls. It will have benefited by some of the intelligence and wealth we lavish to-day on rangefinders and submarines.

Even a village school will be in a beautiful little

building costing as much perhaps as a big naval gun or a bombing-aeroplane costs to-day. I know this will sound like shocking extravagance to many contemporary hearers, but in the World State the standards will be different.

I don't know whether any of us really grasp what we are saying when we talk of greater educational efficiency in the future. That means—if it means anything—teaching more with much less trouble. It will mean, for instance, that most people will have three or four languages properly learnt; that they will think about things mathematical with a quickness and clearness that puzzles us; that about all sorts of things their minds will move in daylight where ours move in a haze of ignorance or in an emotional fog.

This clear-headed, broad-thinking young citizen of the World State will not be given up after his educational years to a life of toil—there will be very little toil left in the world. Mankind will have machines and power enough to do most of the toil for it. Why, between 1914 and 1918 we blew away enough energy and destroyed enough machinery and turned enough good grey matter into stinking filth to release hundreds of millions of toilers from toil for ever!

Our young citizen will choose some sort of interesting work—perhaps creative work. And he will be free to travel about the whole world without a passport or visa, without a change of money; everywhere will be his country; he will find people everywhere who will be endlessly different, but none suspicious or hostile. Everywhere he will find beautiful and distinctive cities, freely expressive of the spirit of the land in which they have arisen. Strange and yet friendly cities.

The world will be a far healthier place than it is now—for mankind as a whole will still carry on organized wars—no longer wars of men against men, but of men against malarias and diseases and infections. Probably he will never know what a cold is, or a headache. He will be able to go through the great forests of the tropics without shivering with fever and without saturating himself with preventive drugs. He will go freely among great mountains; he will fly to the Poles of the earth if he chooses, and dive into the cold, now hidden, deep places of the sea.

But it is very difficult to fill in the picture of his adult life so that it will seem real to our experience. It is hard to conceive and still more difficult to convey. We live in this congested, bickering, elbowing, shoving world, and it has soaked into our natures and made us a part of itself. Hardly any of us know what it is to be properly educated, and hardly any what it is to be in constant general good health.

To talk of what the world may be to most of us is like talking of baths and leisure and happy things to some poor hopeless, gin-soaked drudge in a slum. The creature is so devitalized; the dirt is so ingrained, so much a second nature, that a bath really isn't attractive. Clean and beautiful clothes sound like a mockery or priggishness. To talk of spacious and beautiful places only arouses a violent desire in the poor thing to get away somewhere and hide. In squalor and misery, quarrelling and fighting make a sort of nervous relief. To multitudes of slum-bred people the prospect of no more fighting is a disagreeable prospect, a dull outlook.

Well, all this world of ours may seem a slum to the people of a happier age. They will feel about our world just as we feel about the ninth or tenth century, when we read of its brigands and its insecurities, its pestilences, its miserable housing, its abstinence from ablutions.

But our young citizen will not have been inured to our base world. He will have little of our ingrained dirt in his mind and heart. He will love. He will love beautifully. As most of us once hoped to do in our more romantic moments. He will have ambitions—for the World State will give great scope to ambition. He will work skilfully and brilliantly, or he will administer public services, or he will be an able teacher, or a mental or physical physician, or he will be an interpretative or creative artist; he may be a writer or a scientific investigator, he may be a statesman in his state, or even a world statesman. If he is a statesman he may be going up perhaps to the federal world congress. In the year 2020 there will still be politics, but they will be great politics. Instead of the world's affairs being managed in a score of foreign offices, all scheming meanly and cunningly against each other, all planning to thwart and injure each other, they will be managed under the direction of an educated and organized common intelligence intent only upon the common good.

Dear! Dear! Dear! Does it sound like rubbish to you? I suppose it does. You think I am talking of a dreamland, of an unattainable Utopia? Perhaps I am! This dear, jolly old world of dirt, war, bankruptcy, murder and malice, thwarted lives, wasted lives, tormented lives, general ill health and a social decadence that spreads and deepens towards a universal smash—how can we hope to turn it back from its course? How priggish and impracticable! How impertinent! How preposterous! I seem to hear a distant hooting. . . .

Sometimes it seems to me that the barriers that separate man and man are nearly insurmountable and invincible, that we who talk of a World State now are only the pioneers of a vast uphill struggle in the minds and hearts of men that may need to be waged for centuries—that may fail in the end.

Sometimes again, in other moods, it seems to me that these barriers and nationalities and separations are so illogical, so much a matter of tradition, so plainly mischievous and cruel, that at any time we may find the common sense of our race dissolving them away. . . .

Who can see into that darkest of all mysteries, the hearts and wills of mankind? It may be that

it is well for us not to know of the many generations who will have to sustain this conflict.

Yes, that is one mood, and there is the other.
Perhaps we fear too much. Even before our lives
run out we may feel the dawn of a greater age
perceptible among the black shadows and artificial
glares of these unhappy years.

IV

Part One

§ 1

In my next two papers I am going to discuss and —what shall I say?—experiment with an old but neglected idea, an idea that was first broached I believe about the time when the State of Connecticut was coming into existence and while New York was still the Dutch City of New Amsterdam.

The man who propounded this idea was a certain great Bohemian, Komensky, who is perhaps better known in our western world by his Latinized name Comenius. He professed himself the pupil of Bacon. He was the friend of Milton. He travelled from one European country to another with his political and educational ideas. For a time he thought of coming to America. It is a great pity that he never came. And his idea, the particular idea of his we are going to discuss, was the idea of a common book, a book of history, science and wisdom, which should form the basis and framework for the thoughts and imaginations of every citizen in the world.

97

In many ways the thinkers and writers of the early seventeenth century seem more akin to us and more sympathetic with the world of to-day, than any intervening group of literary figures. They strike us as having a longer vision than the men of the eighteenth century, and as being bolder —and, how shall I put it?—more desperate in their thinking than the nineteenth century minds. And this closer affinity to our own time arises, I should think, directly and naturally, out of the closer resemblance of their circumstances. Between 1640 and 1650, just as in our present age, the world was tremendously unsettled and distressed. A century and more of expansion and prosperity had given place to a phase of conflict, exhaustion, and entire political unsettlement. Britain was involved in the bitter political struggle that culminated in the execution of King Charles I. Ireland was a land of massacre and counter-massacre. The Thirty Years' War in Central Europe was in its closing, most dreadful stages of famine and plunder. In France the crown and the nobles were striving desperately for ascendancy in the War of the Fronde. The Turk threatened Vienna. Nowhere in Western Europe did there remain any secure and settled political arrangements. Everywhere there was disorder, everywhere it seemed that anything might happen, and it is just those disordered and indeterminate times that are most fruitful of bold religious and social and political and educational speculations and initiatives.

This was the period that produced the Quakers

and a number of the most vigorous developments of Puritanism, in which the foundations of modern republicanism were laid, and in which the project of a world league of nations—or rather of a world state—received wide attention. And the student of Comenius will find in him an active and sensitive mind responding with a most interesting similarity to our own responses, to the similar conditions of his time. He has been distressed and dismayed —as most of us have been distressed and dismayed —by a rapid development of violence, by a great release of cruelty and suffering in human affairs. He felt none of the security that was felt in the eighteenth and nineteenth centuries of the *certainty* of progress. He realized as we do that the outlook for humanity is a very dark and uncertain one unless human effort is stimulated and organized. He traced the evils of his time to human discords and divisions, to our political divisions, and the mutual misconceptions due to our diversity of languages and leading ideas. In all that he might be writing and thinking in 1921. And his proposed remedies find an echo in a number of our contemporary movements. He wanted to bring all nations to form one single state. He wanted to have a universal language as the common medium of instruction and discussion, and he wanted to create a common Book of Necessary Knowledge, a sort of common basis of wisdom, for all educated men in the world.

Now this last is the idea I would like to develop now. I would like to discuss whether our education—which nowadays in our modern states reaches everyone—whether our education can include and ought to include such a Book of Necessary Knowledge and Wisdom; and (having attempted to answer that enquiry in the affirmative) I shall then attempt a sketch of such a book.

But to begin with perhaps I may meet an objection that is likely to arise. I have called this hypothetical book of ours the Bible of Civilization, and it may be that someone will say: Yes, but you have a sufficient book of that sort already; you have the Bible itself and that is all you need. Well, I am taking the Bible as my model. I am taking it because twice in history—first as the Old Testament and then again as the Old and New Testament together—it has formed a culture, and unified and kept together through many generations great masses of people. It has been the basis of the Jewish and Christian civilizations alike. And even in the New World the State of Connecticut did, I believe, in its earliest beginnings take the Bible as its only law. Nevertheless, I hope I shall not offend any reader, if I point out that the Bible is not all that we need to-day, and that also in some respects it is redundant. Its very virtues created its limitations. It served men so well that they made a Canon of it and refused to alter it further. Throughout the most vital phases of Hebrew history, throughout the most living years of Christian development the Bible changed and grew. Then its growth ceased and its text became fixed. But the world went on growing and discovering new needs and new necessities.

Let me deal first with its redundancy. So far as redundancy goes, a great deal of the Book of Leviticus, for example, seems not vitally necessary for the ordinary citizen of to-day; there are long explicit directions for temple worship and sacrificial procedure. There is again, so far as the latter day citizen is concerned, an excess of information about the minor Kings of Israel and Judah. And there is more light than most of us feel we require nowadays upon the foreign policies of Assyria and Egypt. It stirs our pulses feebly, it helps us only very indirectly to learn that Attai begat Nathan and Nathan begat Zabad, or that Obed begat Jehu and Jehu begat Azariah, and so on for two or three hundred verses.

And so far as deficiencies go, there is a great multitude of modern problems—problems that enter intimately into the moral life of all of us, with which the Bible does not deal, the establishment of American Independence, for example, and the age-long feud of Russia and Poland that has gone on with varying fortunes for four centuries. That is much more important to our modern world than the ancient conflict of Assyria and Egypt which plays so large a part in the old Bible record. And there are all sorts of moral problems arising out of modern conditions on which the Bible sheds little or no direct light; the duties of a citizen at an election, or the duties of a shareholder to the labour employed by his company, for example.

For these things we need at least a supplement, if we are still to keep our community upon one general basis of understanding, upon one unifying standard of thought and behaviour.

We are so brought up upon the Bible, we are so used to it long before we begin to think hard about it, that all sorts of things that are really very striking about it, the facts that the history of Judah and Israel is told twice over and that the gospel narrative is repeated four times over for example, do not seem at all odd to us. How else, we ask, could you have it? Yet these are very odd features if we are to regard the Bible as the compactest and most perfect statement of essential truth and wisdom.

And still more remarkable, it seems to me, is it that the Bible breaks off. One could understand very well if the Bible broke off with the foundation of Christianity. Now this event has happened, it might say, nothing else matters. It is the culmination. But the Bible does not do that. It goes on to a fairly detailed account of the beginnings and early politics of the Christian Church. It gives the opening literature of theological exposition. And then, with that strange and doubtful book, the Revelation of St. John the Divine, it comes to an end. As I say, it leaves off. It leaves off in the middle of Roman imperial and social conflicts. But the world has gone on and goes on—elaborating its problems, encountering fresh problems—until now there is a gulf of upwards of eighteen hundred years between us and the concluding expression of the thought of that ancient time.

I make these observations in no spirit of detraction. If anything, these peculiarities of the Bible add to the wonder of its influence over the lives and minds of men. It has been The Book that has held together the fabric of western civilization. It has been the handbook of life to countless millions of men and women. The civilization we possess could not have come into existence and could not have been sustained without it. It has explained the world to the mass of our people, and it has given them moral standards and a form into which their consciences could work. But does it do that to-day? Frankly, I do not think it does. I think that during the last century the Bible has lost much of its former hold. It no longer grips the community. And I think it has lost hold because of those sundering eighteen centuries, to which every fresh year adds itself, because of profound changes in the methods and mechanisms of life, and because of the vast extension of our ideas by the development of science in the last century or so.

It has lost hold, but nothing has arisen to take its place. That is the gravest aspect of this matter. It was the cement with which our western communities were built and by which they were held together. And the weathering of these centuries and the acids of these later years have eaten into its social and personal influence. It is no longer a sufficient cement. And—this is the essence of what I am driving at—*our modern communities are no longer cemented,* they lack organized solidarity, they are not prepared to stand shocks and strains, they have become dangerously loose mentally and morally. That, I believe, is the clue to a great proportion of the present social and political troubles of the world. We need to get back to a cement. We want a Bible. We want a Bible so badly that we cannot afford to put the old Bible on a pinnacle out of daily use. We want it re-adapted for use. If it is true that the old Bible falls short in its history and does not apply closely to many modern problems, then we need a revised and enlarged Bible in our schools and homes to restore a common ground of ideas and interpretations if our civilization is to hold together.

Now let us see what the Bible gave a man in the days when it could really grip and hold and contain him; and let us ask if it is impossible to restore and reconstruct a Bible for the needs of these great and dangerous days in which we are living. Can we re-cement our increasingly unstable civilization? I will not ask now whether there is still time left for us to do anything of the sort.

The first thing the Bible gave a man was a Cosmogony. It gave him an account of the world in which he found himself and of his place in it. And then it went on to a general history of mankind. It did not tell him that history as a string of facts and dates, but as a moving and interesting story

into which he himself finally came, a story of
promises made and destinies to be fulfilled. It
gave him a dramatic relationship to the schemes
of things. It linked him to all mankind with a
conception of relationships and duties. It gave
him a place in the world and put a meaning into
his life. It explained him to himself and to other
people, and it explained other people to him. In
other words, out of the individual it made a citizen
with a code of duties and expectations.

Now I take it that both from the point of
view of individual happiness and from the point
of view of the general welfare, this development
of the citizenship of a man, this placing of a man
in his own world, is of primary importance. It is
the necessary basis of all right education; it is
the fundamental purpose of the school, and I do
not believe an individual can be happy or a community be prosperous without it. The Bible and
the religions based on it, gave that idea of a place
in the world to the people it taught. But do we
provide that idea of a place in the world for our
people to-day? I suggest that we do not. We
do not give them a clear vision of the universe
in which they live, and we do not give them a
history that invests their lives with meaning and
dignity.

The cosmogony of the Bible has lost grip and
conviction upon men's minds, and the ever-widen-
ing gulf of years makes its history and its political
teaching more and more remote and unhelpful
amidst the great needs of to-day. Nothing has

been done to fill up these widening gaps. We
have so great a respect for the letter of the Bible
that we ignore its spirit and its proper use. We
do not rewrite and retell Genesis in the light and
language of modern knowledge, and we do not
revise and bring its history up to date and so apply
it to the problems of our own time. So we have
allowed the Bible to become antiquated and remote, venerable and unhelpful.

There has been a great extension of what we call
education in the past hundred years, but while we
have spread education widely, there has been a
sort of shrinkage and enfeeblement of its aims.
Education in the past set out to make a Christian
and a citizen and afterwards a gentleman out of
the crude, vulgar, self-seeking individual. Does
education even pretend to do as much to-day? It
does nothing of the sort. Our young people are
taught to read and write. They are taught book-
keeping and languages that are likely to be useful
to them. They are given a certain measure of
technical education, and *they are taught to shove.*
And then we turn them out into the world to get
on. Our test of a college education is—Does it
make a successful business man?

Well, this, I take it, is the absolute degradation
of education. It is a modern error that education
exists for the individual. Education exists for
the community and the race; it exists to subdue the
individual for the good of the world and his own
ultimate happiness.

But we have been letting the essentials of educa-

tion slip back into a secondary place in our pur-
suit of mere equipment, and we see the results
to-day throughout all the modern states of the
world, in a loss of cohesion, discipline and co-
operation. Men will not co-operate except to raise
prices on the consumer or wages on the employer,
and everyone scrambles for a front place and a
good time. And they do so, partly no doubt by
virtue of an ineradicable factor in them known as
Original Sin, but also very largely because the
vision of life that was built up in their minds at
school and in their homes was fragmentary and
uninspiring; it had no commanding appeal for
their imaginations, and no imperatives for their
lives.

So I put it, that for the opening books of our
Bible of Civilization, our Bible translated into
terms of modern knowledge, and as the basis of
all our culture, we shall follow the old Bible precedent exactly. We shall tell to every citizen of
our community, as plainly, simply and beautifully
as we can, the New Story of Genesis, the tremendous spectacle of the Universe that science has
opened to us, the flaming beginnings of our world,
the vast ages of its making and the astounding
unfolding, age after age, of Life. We shall tell of
the changing climates of this spinning globe and
the coming and going of great floras and faunas,
mighty races of living things, until out of the
vast, slow process our own kind emerged. And
we shall tell the story of our race. How through
hundreds of thousands of years it won power over

nature, hunted and presently sowed and reaped. How it learnt the secrets of the metals, mastered the riddle of the seasons, and took to the seas. That story of our common inheritance and of our slow upward struggle has to be taught throughout our entire community, in the city slums and in the out-of-the-way farmsteads most of all. By teaching it, we restore again to our people the lost basis of a community, a common idea of their place in space and time.

Then, still following the Bible precedent, we must tell a universal history of man. And though on the surface it may seem to be a very different history from the Bible story, in substance it will really be very much the same history, only robbed of ancient trappings and symbols, and made real and fresh again for our present ideas. It will still be a story of conditional promises, the promises of human possibility, a record of sins and blunders and lost opportunities, of men who walked not in the ways of righteousness, of stiff-necked generations, and of merciful renewals of hope. It will still point our lives to a common future which will be the reward and judgment of our present lives.

You may say that no such book exists—which is perfectly true—and that no such book could be written. But there I think you underrate the capacity of our English-speaking people. It would be quite possible to get together a committee that would give us the compact and clear cosmogony of history that is needed. Some of the greatest, most inspiring books and documents in the world have been produced by Committees: Magna Carta, the Declaration of Independence, the English Translation of the Bible, and the Prayer Book of the English Church are all the productions of committees, and they are all fine and inspiring compilations. For the last three years I have been experimenting with this particular task, and, with the help of six other people, I have sketched out and published an outline of our world's origins and history to show the sort of thing I mean. That *Outline* is, of course, a corrupting mass of faults and minor inaccuracies, but it does demonstrate the possibility of doing what is required. And its reception both in America and England has shown how ready, how greedy many people are, on account of themselves and on account of their children, for an ordered general account of the existing knowledge of our place in space and time. For want of anything better they have taken my *Outline* very eagerly. Far more eagerly would they have taken a finer, sounder and more authoritative work.

In England this *Outline* was almost the first experiment of the kind that has been made—the only other I know of in England, was a very compact General History of the World by Mr. Oscar Browning published in 1913. But there are several educationists in America who have been at work on the same task. In this matter of a more generalized history teaching, the New World is decidedly leading the Old. The particular prob-

lems of a population of mixed origins have forced
it upon teachers in the United States.

My friend—I am very happy to be able to call
him my friend—Professor Breasted, in conjunc-
tion with that very able teacher Professor
Robinson, has produced two books, "Ancient
Times" and "Mediæval and Modern Times,"
which together make a very complete history of
civilized man. They do not, however, give a history of life before man, nor very much of human
pre-history. Another admirable American sum-
mary of history is Doctor Hutton Webster's "History of the Ancient World" together with his
"Mediæval and Modern History." This again is
very sparing of the story of primitive man.

But the work of these gentlemen confirms my
own experience that it is quite possible to tell in
a comprehensible and inspiring outline the whole
history of life and mankind in the compass of a
couple of manageable volumes. Neither Browning
nor Breasted and Robinson, nor Hutton Webster,
nor my own effort are very much longer than
twice the length of Dickens' novel of "Bleak
House." So there you have it. There is the thing
shown to be possible. If it is possible for us
isolated workers to do as much, then why should
not the thing be done in a big and authoritative
manner? Why should we not have a great educational conference of teachers, scientific men and
historians from all the civilized peoples of the
world, and why should they not draft out a standard World History for general use in the world's

schools? Why should that draft not be revised by scores of specialists? Discussed and re-discussed? Polished and finished, and made the opening part of a new Bible of Civilization, a new common basis for a world culture?

At intervals it would need to be revised,. and it could be revised and brought up to date in the same manner.

Now such a book and such a book alone would put the people of the world upon an absolutely new footing with regard to social and international affairs. They would be told a history coming right up to the Daily Newspaper. They would see themselves and the news of to-day as part of one great development. It would give their lives significance and dignity. It would give the events of the current day significance and dignity. It would lift their imaginations up to a new level. I say lift, but I mean restore their imaginations to a former level. Because if you look back into the lives of the Pilgrim Fathers, let us say, or into those of the great soldiers and statesmen of Cromwellian England, you will find that these men had a sense of personal significance, a sense of destiny, such as no one in politics or literature seems to possess to-day. They were still in touch with the old Bible. To-day if life seems adventurous and fragmentary and generally aimless it is largely because of this one thing. We have lost touch with history. We have ceased to see human affairs as one great epic unfolding. And only by the universal teaching of Universal History can that epic quality be restored.

You see then the first part of my project for a Bible of Civilization, a rewriting of Genesis and Exodus and Judges and Chronicles in terms of World History. It would be a quite possible thing to do. . . .

Is it worth doing?

And let me add here that when we do get our New Genesis and our new historical books, they will have a great number of illustrations as a living and necessary part of them. For nowadays we can not only have a canonical text, but canonical maps and illustrations. The old Hebrew Bible was merely the written word. Indeed it was not even that, for it was written without vowels. That was not a merit, nor a precedent for us; it was an unavoidable limitation in those days; but under modern conditions there is no reason whatever why we should confine our Bible to words when a drawing or a map can better express the thing we wish to convey. It is one of the great advantages of the modern book over the ancient book that because of printing it can use pictures as well as words. When books had to be reproduced by copyists the use of pictures was impossible. They would have varied with each copying until they became hopelessly distorted. . . .

But the cosmological and historical part of the old Bible was merely the opening, the groundwork upon which the rest was built. Let us now consider what else the Bible gave a man and a community, and what would be the modern form of the things it gave.

The next thing in order that the Bible gave a man and the community to which he belonged, was the Law. Rules of Life. Rules of Health. Prescriptions—often very detailed and intimate—of permissible and unpermissible conduct. This also the modern citizen needs and should have: he and she need a book of personal wisdom.

First as to Health. One of the first duties of a citizen is to keep himself in mental and bodily health in order to be fit for the rest of his duties. Now the real Bible, our model, is extremely explicit upon a number of points, upon what constitutes cleanness or uncleanness, upon ablutions, upon what a man or woman may eat and what may not be eaten, upon a number of such points. It was for its times and circumstances a directory of healthy practice. Well, I do not see why the Bible of a Modern Civilization should not contain a book of similarly clear injunctions and warnings

—why we should not tell every one of our people what is to be known about self-care.

And closely connected with the care of one's mental and bodily health is sexual morality, upon which again Deuteronomy and Leviticus are most explicit, leaving very little to the imagination. I am all for imitating the wholesome frankness of the ancient book. Where there are no dark corners there is very little fermentation, there is very little foulness or infection. But in nearly every detail and in method and manner, the Bible of our Civilization needs to be fuller and different from its prototype upon these matters. The real Bible dealt with an oriental population living under much cruder conditions than our own, engaged mainly in agriculture, and with a far less varied dietary than ours. They had fermented but not distilled liquors; they had no preserved nor refrigerated foods; they married at adolescence; many grave diseases that prevail to-day were unknown to them, and their sanitary problems were entirely different. Generally our New Leviticus will have to be much fuller. It must deal with exercise—which came naturally to those Hebrew shepherds. It must deal with the preservation of energy under conditions of enervation of which the prophets knew nothing. On the other hand our New Leviticus can afford to give much less attention to leprosy—which almost dominates the health instructions of the ancient law-giver.

I do not know anything very much about the movements in America that aim at the improvement of the public health and at the removal of public ignorance upon vital things. In Britain we have a number of powerful organizations active in disseminating knowledge to counteract the spread of this or that infectious or contagious disease. The War has made us in Europe much more outspoken and fearless in dealing with lurking hideous evils. We believe much more than we did in the curative value of light and knowledge. And we have a very considerable literature of books on —what shall I call it?—on Sex Wisdom, which aim to prevent some of that great volume of misery, deprivation and nervous disease due to the prevailing ignorance and secrecy in these matters. For in these matters great multitudes of modern people still live in an ignorance that would have been inconceivable to an ancient Hebrew. In England now the books of such a writer as Dr. Marie Stopes are enormously read, and—though they are by no means perfect works—do much to mitigate the hidden disappointments, discontents, stresses and cruelties of married life. Now I believe that it would be possible to compile a modern Leviticus and Deuteronomy to tell our whole modern community decently and plainly—just as plainly as the old Hebrew Bible instructed its Hebrew population—what was to be known and what had to be done, and what had not to be done in these intimate matters.

But Health and Sex do not exhaust the problems of conduct. There are also the problems of Property and Trade and Labour. Upon these

also the old Bible did not hesitate to be explicit.
For example, it insisted meticulously upon the
right of labour to glean and upon the seller giving
a "full measure brimming over," and it prohibited
usury. But here again the Bible is extraordinarily
unhelpful when we come to modern issues, because
its rules and regulations were framed for a community and for an economic system altogether
cruder, more limited and less complicated than our
own. Much of the Old Testament we have to
remember was already in existence before the free
use of coined metal. The vast credit system of
our days, joint-stock company enterprise and the
like, were beyond the imagination of that time. So
too was any anticipation of modern industrialism.
And accordingly we live to-day in a world in which
neither property nor employment have ever been
properly moralized. The bulk of our present
social and economic troubles is due very largely
to that.

In no matter is this muddled civilization of ours
more hopelessly at sixes and sevens than in this
matter of the rights and duties of property. Manifestly property is a trust for the community varying in its responsibilities with the nature of the
property. The property one has in one's tooth-
brush is different from the property one has in ten
thousand acres of land; the property one has in a
photograph of a friend is different from the property one has in some irreplaceable masterpiece of
portraiture, The former one may destroy with

a good conscience, but not the latter. At least so it seems to me.

But opinions vary enormously on these matters because we have never really worked them out. On the one hand, in this matter of property, we have the extreme individualist who declares that a man has an unlimited right to do what he likes with his own—so that a man who owns a coal mine may just burn it out to please himself or spite the world, or raise the price of coal generally—and on the other hand we have the extreme communist who denies all property and in practice—so far as I can understand his practice—goes on the principle that everything belongs to somebody else or that one is entitled to exercise proprietary rights over everything that does not belong to oneself. (I confess that communistic practice is a little difficult to formulate.) Between these extremists you can find every variety of idea about what one may do and about what one may not do with money and credit and property generally. Is it an offence to gamble? Is it an offence to speculate? Is it an offence to hold fertile fields and not cultivate them? Is it an offence to hold fertile fields and undercultivate them? Is it an offence to use your invested money merely to live pleasantly without working? Is it an offence to spend your money on yourself and refuse your wife more than bare necessities? Is it an offence to spend exorbitant sums that might otherwise go in reproductive investments, to gratify the whims and vanities of your wife? You will find different people answering any of these questions with Yes and No. But it cannot be both Yes and No. There must be a definable Right or Wrong upon all these issues.

Almost all the labour trouble in the world springs directly from our lack of an effective detailed moral code about property. The freedom that is claimed for all sorts of property and exercised by all sorts of property to waste or withhold is the clue to that savage resentment which flares out nowadays in every great labour conflict. Labour is a rebel because property is a libertine.

Now this untilled field of conduct, this moral wilderness of the rights and duties and limitations of property, the Books of the Law in a modern Bible could clear up in the most lucid and satisfying way. I want to get those parts of Deuteronomy and Leviticus written again, more urgently than any other part of the modern Bible. I want to see it at work in the schools and in the lawcourts. I admit that it would be a most difficult book to write and that we should raise controversial storms over every verse. But what an excellent thing to have it out, once for all, with some of these rankling problems! What an excellent thing if we could get together a choice group of representative men—strictly rationed as to paper—and get them to set down clearly and exactly just what classes of property they recognized and what limitations the community was entitled to impose upon each sort.

Every country in the world does impose limitations. In Italy you may not export an ancient

work of art, although it is your own. In England‧
you may not maltreat your own dog or cat. In
the United States, I am told, you may not use
your dollars to buy alcohol. Why should we not
make all this classification of property and the
restraints upon each class of property, systematic
and world-wide? If we could so moralize the use
of property, if we could arrive at a clear idea of
just what use an owner could make of his machinery, or a financier could make of his credit, would
there be much left of the incessant labour conflicts
of the present time? For if you will look into it,
you will find there is hardly ever a labour conflict
into which some unsettled question of principle,
some unsettled question of the permissible use of
property, does not enter as the final and essential
dispute.

V

THE BIBLE OF CIVILIZATION

PART TWO

§ 1

In the preceding sections we have discussed Genesis and the Historical Books generally as they would appear in a modernized Bible, and we have dealt with the Law. But these are only the foundations and openings of the Bible as we know it. We come now to the Psalms and Proverbs, the Song of Songs, the Book of Job—and the Prophets. What are the modern equivalents of these books?

Well, what were they?

They were the entire Hebrew literature down to about the time of Ezra; they include sacred songs, love songs, a dramatic dialogue, a sort of novel in the Books of Ruth and Esther, and so forth. What would be our equivalent of this part of the Bible to-day? What would be the equivalent for the Bible of a World Civilization?

I suppose that it would be the whole world literature.

That, I admit, is a rather tremendous proposition. Are we to contemplate the prospect of a modern Bible in twenty or thirty thousand volumes? Such a vast Bible would defeat its own end. We want a Bible that everyone will know, which will be grasped by the mind of everyone. That is essential to our idea of a Bible as a social cement.

Fortunately, our model Bible, as we have it to-day, gives us a lead in this matter. Its contents are classified. We have first of all the canonical books, which are treated as the vitally important books; they are the books, to quote the phrase used in the English prayer book, which are "necessary to salvation." And then we have a collection of other books, the Apocrypha, the books set aside, books often admirable and beautiful, but not essential, good to be read for "example of life and instruction of manners," yet books that everyone need not read and know. Let us take this lead and let us ask whether we can—with the whole accumulated literature of the world as our material—select a bookful or so of matter, of such exceptional value that it would be well for all mankind to read it and know it. This will be our equivalent for the canonical books. I will return to that in a moment.

And outside this canonical book or books, shall we leave all the rest of literature in a limitless Apocrypha? I am doubtful about that. I would suggest that we make a second intermediate class between the canonical books that everyone

in our civilization ought to read and the outer
Apocrypha that you may read or not as you
choose.   This intermediate class I would call the
Great Books of the World.   It would not be a part
of our Bible, but it would come next to our Bible.
It would not be what one must read but only what
it is desirable the people should read.

Now this canonical literature we are discussing
is to be the third vital part of our modern Bible.
I conceive of it as something that would go into the
hands of every man and woman in that coming
great civilization which is the dream of our race.
Together with the Book of World History and the
Book of Law and Righteousness and Wisdom that
I have sketched out to you, and another Book of
which I shall have something to say later, this
Canonical Literature will constitute the intellectual and moral cement of the World Society, that
intellectual and moral cement for the want of
which our world falls into political and social confusion and disaster to-day.   Upon such a basis,
upon a common body of ideas, a common moral
teaching and the world-wide assimilation of the
same emotional and æsthetic material, it may still
be possible to build up humanity into one co-opera-
tive various and understanding community.

Now if we bear this idea of a cementing function firmly in mind, we shall have a criterion by
which to judge what shall be omitted from and
what shall be included in the Books of Literature
in this modern Bible of ours.   We shall begin, of
course, by levying toll upon the Old and New

Testaments. I do not think I need justify that step. I suppose that there will be no doubt of the inclusion of many of the Psalms—but I question if we should include them all—and of a number of splendid passages from the Prophets. Should we include the Song of Songs? I am inclined to think that the compilers of a new Bible would hesitate at that. Should we include the Book of Job? That I think would be a very difficult question indeed for our compilers. The Book of Job is a very wonderful and beautiful discussion of the profound problem of evil in the world. It is a tremendous exercise to read and understand, but is it universally necessary? I am disposed to think that the Book of Job, possibly with the illustrations of Blake, would not make a part of our Canon but would rank among our Great Books. It is a part of a very large literature of discussion, of which I shall have more to say in a moment. So too I question if we should make the story of Ruth or the story of Esther fundamental teaching for our world civilization. Daniel, again, I imagine relegated to the Apocrypha. But to this I will return later.

The story of the Gospels would, of course, have been incorporated in our Historical Book, but in addition as part of our first canon, each of the four gospels—with the possible omission of the genealogies—would have a place, for the sake of their matchless directness, simplicity and beauty. They give a picture, they convey an atmosphere of supreme value to us all, incommunicable in any other form or language. Again there is a great wealth of material in the Epistles. It is, for example, inconceivable that such a passage as that of St. Paul's Epistle to the Corinthians—"Though I speak with the tongues of men and angels and have not charity I am become as sounding brass or a tinkling cymbal"—the whole of that wonderful chapter—should ever pass out of the common heritage of mankind.

So much from the Ancient Bible for our modern Bible, all its inspiration and beauty and fire. And now what else?

Speaking in English to an English-speaking audience one name comes close upon the Bible, Shakespeare. What are we going to do about Shakespeare? If you were to waylay almost any Englishman or American and put this project of a modern Bible before him, and then begin your list of ingredients with the Bible and the whole of Shakespeare, he would almost certainly say, "Yes, yes."

But would he be right?

On reflection he might perhaps recede and say, "Not the whole of Shakespeare," but well, "Hamlet," "The Tempest," "Romeo and Juliet," "The Midsummer Night's Dream." But even these! Are they "generally necessary to salvation"? We run our minds through the treasures of Shakespeare as we might run our fingers through the contents of a box of very precious and beautiful jewels—before equipping a youth for battle.

No. These things are for ornament and joy. I doubt if we could have a single play—a single scene of Shakespeare's in our Canon. He goes altogether into the Great Books, all of him; he joins the aristocracy of the Apocrypha. And, I believe, nearly all the great plays of the world would have to join him there. Euripides and Sophocles, Schiller and Ibsen. Perhaps some speeches and such-like passages might be quoted in the Canon, but that is all.

Our Canon, remember, is to be the essential cementing stuff of our community and nothing more. If once we admit merely beautiful and delightful things, then I see an overwhelming inrush of jewels and flowers. If we admit, "The Midsummer Night's Dream," then I must insist that we also admit such lovely nonsense as

> In Xanadu did Kubla Khan
> A stately pleasure dome decree
> Where Alph the sacred river ran
> Through caverns measureless to man
> Down to a sunless sea. . . .

Our Canon I am afraid cannot take in such things, and with the plays we must banish also all the novels; the greater books of such writers as Cervantes, Defoe, Dickens, Fielding, Tolstoi, Hardy, Hamsun, that great succession of writers —they are all good for "example of life and instruction of manners," and to the Apocrypha they must go. And so it is that since I would banish "Romeo and Juliet," I would also banish the Song of Songs, and since I must put away "Vanity Fair" and the "Shabby Genteel Story,"

I would also put away *Esther* and *Ruth*. And I find
myself most reluctant to exclude not any novels
written in English, but one or two great sweeping
books by non-English writers. It seems to me that
Tolstoi's "War and Peace" and Hamsun's
"Growth of the Soil" are books on an almost
Biblical scale, that they deal with life so greatly as
to come nearest to the idea of a universally inspiring and illuminating literature which under-
lies the idea of our Canon. If we put any whole
novels into the Canon I would plead for these.
But I will not plead now even for these. I do not
think any novels at all can go into our modern
Bible, as whole works. The possibility of long passages going in is, of course, quite a different
matter.

And passing now from great plays and great
novels and romances, we come to the still more
difficult problem of great philosophical and critical
works. Take "Gulliver's Travels," an intense,
dark, stirring criticism of life and social order—
and the "Dialogues of Plato," full of light and inspiration. In these latter we might quarry for
beautiful passages for our Canon, but I do not
think we could take them in as wholes, and if we
do not take them in as complete books, then I think
that Semitic parallel to these Greek dialogues,
The Book of Job, must stand not in our Canon, but
in the Great Book section of our Apocrypha.

And next we have to consider all the great Epics
in the world. There again I am for exclusion. This
Bible we are considering must be universally

available. If it is too bulky for universal use it loses its primary function of a moral cement. We cannot include the "Iliad," the Norse Sagas, the "Æneid," or "Paradise Lost" in our Canon. Let them swell the great sack of our Apocrypha, and let the children read them if they will.

When one glances in this fashion over the accumulated literary resources of mankind it becomes plain that our canonical books of literature in this modern Bible of ours can be little more than an Anthology or a group of Anthologies. Perhaps they might be gathered under separate heads, as the "Book of Freedom," the "Book of Justice," the "Book of Charity." And now having done nothing as yet but reject, let me begin to accept. Let me quote a few samples of the kind of thing that I imagine would best serve the purpose of our Bible and that should certainly be included.

Here are words that every American knows by heart already—I would like every man in the world to know them by heart and to repeat them. It is Lincoln's Gettysburg Address and I will not spare you a word of it:

"Fourscore and seven years ago our fathers brought forth on this continent a new nation, conceived in liberty, and dedicated to the proposition that all men are created equal. Now we are engaged in a great civil war, testing whether that nation, or any nation so conceived and so dedicated, can long endure. We are met on a great battlefield of that war. We have come to dedi-

cate a portion of that field, as a final resting-place
for those who here gave their lives that that nation
might live. It is altogether fitting and proper that
we should do this. But in a larger sense, we cannot dedicate—we cannot consecrate—we cannot
hallow—this ground. The brave men, living and
dead, who struggled here, have consecrated it, far
above our poor power to add or detract. The
world will little note, nor long remember what we
say here, but it can never forget what they did
here. It is for us, the living, rather, to be dedicated here to the unfinished work which they who
fought here have thus far so nobly advanced. It
is rather for us to be here dedicated to the great
task remaining before us—that from these hon-
ored dead we take increased devotion to that cause
for which they gave the last full measure of devotion. That we here highly resolve that these
dead shall not have died in vain—that this nation,
under God, shall have a new birth of freedom—
and that Government of the people, by the people,
for the people, shall not perish from the earth.''

And here is something that might perhaps make
another short chapter in the same Book of Freedom—but it deals with Freedom of a different
sort:

> Out of the night that covers me
>   Black as the pit from pole to pole,
> I thank whatever gods may be
>   For my unconquerable soul.
> In the fell clutch of circumstance

I have not winced nor cried aloud,
Under the bludgeonings of Chance,
  My head is bloody but unbowed.

Beyond this Place of wrath and tears,
  Looms but the Horror of the Shade,
And yet the Menace of the years
  Finds and shall find me Unafraid.
It matters not how strait the gate,
  How charged with punishments the scroll,
I am the Master of my Fate,
  I am the Captain of my Soul.

That, as you know was Henley's, and as I
turned up his volume of poems to copy out that
poem I came again on these familiar lines:

The ways of Death are soothing and serene,
  And all the words of Death are grave and sweet,
  From camp and church, the fireside and the street,
She beckons forth—and strife and song have been.

A summer's night descending cool and green,
  And dark on daytime's dust and stress and heat,
The ways of Death are soothing and serene,
  And all the words of Death are grave and sweet.

There seems something in that also which I
could spare only very reluctantly from a new Bible
in the world. Yet I tender those lines very doubt-
fully. For I am not a very cultivated and well-
read person, and note only the things that have
struck upon my mind; but I quite understand that
there must be many things of the same sort, but
better, that I have never encountered, or that I

have not heard or read under circumstances that were favourable to their proper appreciation. I would rather say about what I am quoting in this section, not positively "this thing," but merely "this sort of thing."

And in the vein of "this sort of thing" let me quote you—again for the Book of Freedom—a passage from Milton, defending the ancient English tradition of free speech and free decision and praising London and England. This London and England of which he boasts have broadened out as the idea of Jerusalem has broadened out, to world-wide comprehensions. Let no false modesty blind us to our great tradition; you and I are still thinking in Milton's city; we continue, however unworthily, the great inheritance of the world-wide responsibility and service, of His Englishmen. Here is my passage:

"Now once again by all concurrence of signs, and by the general instinct of holy and devout men, as they daily and solemnly express their thoughts, God is decreeing to begin some new and great period in His Church, even to the reforming of reformation itself; what does He then but reveal Himself to His servants, and as His manner is, first to His Englishmen? I say, as His manner is, first to us, though we mark not the method of His counsels, and are unworthy. Behold now this vast city, a city of refuge, the mansion-house of liberty, encompassed and surrounded with His

protection; the shop of war hath not there more
anvils and hammers working, to fashion out the
plates and instruments of armed justice in defence
of beleaguered truth, than there be pens and heads
there, sitting by their studious lamps, musing,
searching, revolving new notions and ideas where-
with to present, as with their homage and their
fealty, the approaching reformation: others as
fast reading, trying all things, assenting to the
force of reason and convincement.

"What could a man require more from a nation so pliant and so prone to seek after knowledge? What wants there to such a towardly and
pregnant soil, but wise and faithful labourers, to
make a knowing people, a nation of prophets, of
sages, and of worthies? We reckon more than five
months yet to harvest; there need not be five
weeks, had we but eyes to lift up, the fields are
white already. Where there is much desire to
learn, there of necessity will be much arguing,
much writing, many opinions; for opinion in good
men is but knowledge in the making. Under these
fantastic terrors of sect and schism, we wrong the
earnest and zealous thirst after knowledge and
understanding, which God hath stirred up in this
city. What some lament of, we rather should re-
joice at, should rather praise this pious forward-
ness among men, to reassume the ill-deputed care
of their religion into their own hands again. A
little generous prudence, a little forbearance of
one another, and some grain of charity might win

all these diligencies to join and unite into one general and brotherly search after truth; could we but forego this prelatical tradition of crowding free consciences and Christian liberties into canons and precepts of men. I doubt not, if some great and worthy stranger should come among us, wise to discern the mould and temper of a people, and how to govern it, observing the high hopes and aims, the diligent alacrity of our extended thoughts and reasonings in the pursuance of truth and freedom, but that he would cry out as Pyrrhus did, admiring the Roman docility and courage: 'If such were my Epirots, I would not despair the greatest design that could be attempted to make a church or kingdom happy.'

"Yet these are the men cried out against for schismatics and sectaries, as if, while the temple of the Lord was building, some cutting, some squaring the marble, others hewing the cedars, there should be a sort of irrational men, who could not consider there must be many schisms and many dissections made in the quarry and in the timber ere the house of God can be built. And when every stone is laid artfully together, it cannot be united into a continuity, it can but be contiguous in this world: neither can every piece of the building be of one form; nay, rather the perfection consists in this, that out of many moderate varieties and brotherly dissimilitudes that are not vastly disproportional, arises the goodly and the graceful symmetry that commends the whole pile and structure."

But I will not go on turning over the pages of books and reciting prose and poetry to you. I cannot even begin to remind you of the immense treasure of noble and ennobling prose and verse that this world has accumulated in the past three thousand years. Not one soul in ten thousand that is born into this world even tastes from that store. For most of mankind now that treasure is as if it had never been. Is it too much to suggest that we should make some organized attempt to gather up the quintessence of literature now, and make it accessible to the masses of our race? Why should we not on a large scale with a certain breadth and dignity set about compiling the Poetic Books, the Books of Inspiration for a renewed Bible, for a Bible of Civilization? It seems to me that such a Book made universally accessible, made a basis of teaching everywhere, could set the key of the whole world's thought.

4

There remains one other element if we are to complete the parallelism of the old Bible and the new. The Christian Bible ends with a forecast, the Book of Revelation; the Hebrew Bible ended also with forecasts, the *Prophets*. To that the old Bible owed much of its magic power over men's imaginations and the inspiration it gave them. It was not a dead record, not an accumulation of things finished and of songs sung. It pointed steadily and plainly to the Days to Come as the end and explanation of all that went before. So, too, our modern Bible, if it is to hold and rule the imagination of men, must close, I think, with a *Book of Forecasts*.

We want to make our world think more than it does about the consequences of the lives it leads and the political deeds that it does and that it permits to be done. We want to turn the human imagination round again towards the future which our lives create. We want a collection and digest of forecasts and warnings to complete this modern Bible of ours. Now here I think you will say—and I admit with perfect reason—that I am floating away from any reasonable possibility at all. How can we have forecasts and prophecies of things that are happening now? Well, I will make a clean breast of it, and admit that I am asking for something that may be impossible. Nevertheless it is something that is very necessary if men are to remain indeed intelligent co-operating communities. In the past you will find where there have been orderly and successful communities the men in them had an idea of a Destiny, of some object, something that would amount to a criterion and judgment upon their collective conduct. Well, I believe that we have to get back to something of that sort.

We have statesmen and politicians who profess to guide our destinies. Whither are they guiding our destinies?

Surely they have some idea. The great American statesmen and the great European statesmen are making To-morrow. What is the To-morrow they are making?

They must have some idea of it. Otherwise they must be imposters. I am loth to believe them imposters, mere adventurers who have blundered into positions of power and honour with no idea of what they are doing to the world. But if they have an idea of what they are doing to the world, they foresee and intend a Future. That, I take it, is sound reasoning and the inference is plain.

They ought to write down their ideas of this Future before us. It would be helpful to all of us. It might be a very helpful exercise for them. It is, I think, reasonable for Americans to ask the great political personages of America, the president and so forth, for example: whether they think

the United States will stand alone in twenty-five
years' time as they stand alone now? Or whether
they think that there will be a greater United
States—of all America—or of all the world?
They must know their own will about that. And
it is equally reasonable to ask the great political
personages of the British Empire: what will Ireland be in twenty-five years' time? What will
India be? There must be a plan, an intended
thing. Otherwise these men have no intentions;
otherwise they must be, in two words, dangerous
fools. The sooner we substitute a type of man
with a sufficient foresight and capable of articu-
late speech in the matter, the better for our race.

And again every statesman and every politician
throughout the world says that the relations of
industrial enterprise to the labour it employs are
unsatisfactory. Yes. But how are those relations
going to develop? How do they mean them to develop?

Are we just drifting into an unknown darkness
in all these matters with blind leaders of our blind-
ness? Or cannot a lot of these things be figured
out by able and intelligent people? I put it to you
that they can. That it is a reasonable and proper
thing to ask our statesmen and politicians: what
is going to happen to the world? What sort of
better social order are you making for? What
sort of world order are you creating? Let them
open their minds to us, let them put upon per-
manent record the significance of all their in-
trigues and manœuvres. Then as they go on we

can check their capacity and good faith. We can establish a control at last that will rule presidents and kings.

Now the answer to these questions for statesmen is what I mean by a *Book of Forecasts*. Such a book I believe is urgently needed to help our civilization. It is a book we ought all to possess and read. I know you will say that such a *Book of Forecasts* will be at first a preposterously insufficient book—that every year will show it up and make it more absurd. I quite agree. The first *Book of Forecasts* will be a poor thing. Miserably poor. So poor that people will presently clamour to have it thoroughly revised.

The revised *Book of Forecasts* will not be quite so bad. It will have been tested against realities. It will form the basis of a vast amount of criticism and discussion.

When again it comes to be revised, it will be much nearer possible realities.

I put it to you that the psychology, the mentality of a community that has a *Book of Forecasts* in hand and under watchful revision will be altogether steadier and stronger and clearer than that of a community which lives as we do to-day, mere adventurers, without foresight, in a world of catastrophes and accidents and unexpected things. We shall be living again in a plan. Our lives will be shaped to certain defined ends. We shall fall into place in a great scheme of activities. We shall recover again some or all of the steadfastness and dignity of the old religious life.

5

Let me with this *Book of Forecasts* round off my fantasy. I would picture to you this modern Bible, perhaps two or three times as bulky as the old Bible, and consisting first of

The Historical Books with maps and the like;

The Books of Conduct and Wisdom;

The Anthologies of Poetry and Literature; and finally, the

Book of Forecasts, taking the place of the Prophets and Revelations.

I would picture this revivified Bible to you as most carefully done and printed and made accessible to all, the basis of education in every school, the common platform of all discussion—just as in the past the old Bible used to be. I would ask you to imagine it translated into every language, a common material of understanding throughout all the world.

And furthermore, I imagine something else about this—quite unlike the old Bible—I imagine all of it periodically revised. The historical books would need to be revised and brought up to date, there would be new lights on health and conduct, there would be fresh additions to the anthologies, and there would be Forecasts that would have to be struck out because they were realized or

because they were shown to be hopeless or un-
desirable, and fresh Forecasts would be added to
replace them. It would be a Bible moving forward and changing and gaining with human experience and human destiny. . . .

Well, that is my dream of a Bible of Civilization. Have I in any way carried my vision out
to you of this little row of four or five volumes in
every house, in every life, throughout the world,
holding the lives and ideas* and imaginations of
men together in a net of common familiar phrases
and common established hopes?

And is this a mere fantastic talk, or is this a
thing that could be done and that ought to be done?

I do not know how it will appear to you, but
to me it seems that this book I have been talking
about, the Bible of to-day's civilization, is not
simply a conceivable possibility, it is a great and
urgent need. Our education is, I think, pointless
without it, a shell without a core. Our social life
is aimless without it, we are a crowd without a
common understanding. Only by means of some
such unifying instrument, I believe, can we hope
to lift human life out of its present dangerous drift
towards confusion and disaster.

It is, I think therefore, an urgently desirable
undertaking.

It is also a very practicable one. The creation
of such a Bible, its printing and its translation,
and a propaganda that would carry it into the
homes and schools of most of the world, could I
think all be achieved by a few hundred resolute

and capable people at a cost of thirty or forty million dollars. That is a less sum than that the United States—in a time when they have no enemy to fear in all the world—are prepared to spend upon the building of what is for them an entirely superfluous and extravagant toy, a great navy.

You may, you probably will, differ very widely upon much that I have here put before you. Let me ask you not to let any of the details of my sketching set you against the fundamental idea, that old creative idea of the Bohemian educationist who was the pupil of Bacon and the friend of Milton, the idea of Komensky, the idea of creating and using a common book, a book of knowledge and wisdom, as the necessary foundation for any enduring human unanimity.

VI

THE SCHOOLING OF THE WORLD

AND now I am going on to a review of the broad facts of the educational organization of our present world.

I am myself a very undereducated person. It is a constant trouble to me. Like seeks like in this world. I propose to ask the question whether the whole world is not undereducated, and I warn you in advance that I am going to answer in the affirmative.

I am going to discuss the possibility of raising the general educational level very considerably, and I am going to consider what such a raising of the educational level would mean in human life.

I propose to adopt rather a vulgar, businesslike tone about all this. I am going to apply to the human community much the same sort of tests that a manufacturer applies to his factory. His factory has some distinctive product, and when he looks into his affairs he tries to find out whether he gets the best possible quality of the product, whether he gets it as efficiently and inexpensively as possible, and constantly how he can improve his factory and his processes in all these matters.

Now the human community may be regarded as

a concern engaged in the production of human life. And it may be judged very largely by the question whether the human life it produces is abundant and full and intense and beautiful.

Most of the tests that we apply to a state or a city or a period or a nation resolve themselves, you will find, into these questions:—

What was the life it produced?

What is the life it produces?

Now I will further assume that as yet the community has little or no control over the raw product, over the life, that is to say, that comes into it. I admit that from at least the time of Plato onward the possibility has been discussed of *breeding* human beings as we do horses and dogs. There is an enormous amount of what is called eugenic literature and discussion to-day. But I will set all that sort of thing aside from our present discussion because I do not think anything of the kind is practicable at the present time.

Quite apart from any other considerations, one has to remember one entire difference between the possible breeding of human beings and the actual breeding of dogs and horses. We breed dogs and horses for uniformity, for certain very limited specified *points*—speed, scent and the like. But human beings we should have to breed for variety: we cannot specify any particular *points* we want. We want statesmen and poets and musicians and philosophers and swift men and strong men and delicate men and brave men. The qualities of one would be the weaknesses of another.

It is really a false analogy, that between the breeding of men and the breeding of horses and dogs. In the case of human beings we want much more subtle and delicate combinations of qualities. For any practical purposes we do not know what we want nor do we know how to get it. So let us rule that theme out of our present discussion altogether.

And I also propose to rule out another set of topics from this discussion—simply because if we don't do so we shall have more matter than we can handle conveniently in the time at our disposal. I propose to leave out all questions of health and physical welfare. There is, as you know, a vast literature now in existence, concerned with the health and welfare of children before and after birth, concerned with infantile life, with social conditions and social work directed to the production of a vigorous population. I am going to assume here that all that sort of thing is seen to —that it is all right, that somebody is doing that, that we need not trouble for the present about any of those things.

This leaves us with the mental life only of our community and its individuals to consider. On that I propose to concentrate this discussion.

Now the human mind in its opening stages in a civilized community passes through a process which may best be named as *schooling*. And under schooling I would include not only the sort of things that we do to a prospective citizen in the school and the infant school but also anything in the nature of a school-like lesson that is done by the mother or nurse or tutor at home, or by playmates and companions anywhere. Out of this schooling arises the general mental life. It is the structural ground-stuff of all education and thought.

Now what is this *schooling* to do—what is it doing to the new human being?

Let us recall what our own schooling was.

It fell into two pretty clearly defined parts. We learnt reading and writing, we made a certain study of grammar, the method of language, perhaps we learnt the beginnings of some other language than our own; we learnt some arithmetic and perhaps a little geometry and algebra; we did some drawing. All these things were ways of expression, means of expressing ourselves, means of comprehending our thoughts in terms of other people's minds, and of understanding the expressions of others. That was the basis and substance of our schooling; a training in mental elucidation and in communication with other minds. But also as our schooling went on there was something more; we learnt a little history, some geography, the beginnings of science. This second part of education was not so much expression as *wisdom*. We learnt what was generally known of the world about us and of its past. We entered into the common knowledge and common ideas of the world.

Now, obviously, this *schooling* is merely a specialization and expansion of a parental function.

In the primitive ages of our race the parent,

and particularly the mother, out of an instinctive impulse and practical necessity, restrained and showed and taught, and the child, with an instinctive imitativeness and docility, obeyed and learnt. And as the primitive family grew into a tribe, as functions specialized and the range of knowledge widened, this primitive schooling by the mother was supplemented and extended by the showing of things by companions and by the maxims and initiations of old men.

It was only with the development of early civilizations, as the mysteries of writing and reading began to be important in life, that the school, *qua* school, became a thing in itself. And as the community expanded, the scope of instruction expanded with it. Schooling is, in fact, and always has been, the expansion and development of the primitive savage mind, which is still all that we inherit, to adapt it to the needs of a larger community. It makes out of the savage raw material which is our basal mental stuff, a citizen. It is a necessary process of fusion if a civilized community is to keep in being. Without at least a network of schooled persons, able to communicate its common ideas and act in intelligent co-operation, no community beyond a mere family group can ever hold together.

As the human community expands, therefore, the range of schooling must expand to keep pace with it.

I want to base my enquiry upon that proposition. If it is sound, certain very interesting conclusions follow.

I have already shown in the preceding discussions that the *range* of the modern state has increased at least ten times in the past century, and that the scale of our community of intercourse has increased correspondingly. I want now to ask if there has been any corresponding enlargement of the scope of the schooling—either of the community as a whole or of any special governing classes in the community—to keep pace with this tremendous extension of range. I am going to argue that there has not been such an enlargement, and that a large factor in our present troubles is the failure of education and educational method to keep pace with the new demands made upon them.

Now I will first ask what would one like one's son or daughter to get at school to make him or her a full living citizen of this modern world. And at first I will not take into consideration the question of expense or any such practical difficulties. I will suppose that for the education of this fortunate young citizen whose case we are considering we have limitless means, the best possible tutors, the best apparatus and absolutely the most favourable conditions. The only limits to the teaching of this young citizen are his or her own limitations. We suppose a pupil of fair average intelligence only.

Now first we shall want our pupil to understand, speak, read and write the mother tongue well. To do this thoroughly in English involves a fairly sound knowledge of Latin grammar and at least some slight knowledge of the elements of Greek. Latin and Greek, which are disappearing as distinct and separate subjects from many school curricula, are returning as necessary parts of the English course.

But nowadays a full life is not to be lived with a single language. The world becomes polyglot. Even if we do not want to live among foreigners, we want to read their books and newspapers and understand and follow their thought. Few of us there are how would not gladly read and speak several more languages if we had the chance of doing so. I would therefore set down as a desirable part of this ideal education we are planning, two or three other languages in addition to the mother tongue learnt early and thoroughly. These additional languages can be acquired easily if they are learnt in the right way. The easiest way to learn a language is to learn it when you are quite young. Many prosperous people in Europe nowadays contrive to bring up their children with two or three foreign languages, by employing foreign nurses and nursery governesses who never speak to the children except in the foreign languages. In many cases what is known as the alternate week system prevails. The governess is Swiss and for one week she talks nothing but French and for another nothing but German. In this way the children at the age of eight or nine can be made to talk all three languages with a perfect accent and an easy idiom.

Now if this can be done for some children it could be done for all children—provided we could find the nurses and governesses or some equivalent for the nurses and governesses, and if we can organize the business efficiently. That point I will defer. I note here simply that the thing is possible, if not practicable.

Children, however, who have made this much start with languages are unable in England and America, at least, to go on properly with the learning of languages when they pass into a school. Our schools are so badly organized that it is rare to find even French well taught, and there is rarely any teaching at all of modern languages other than French or German. Often the two foreign languages are taught by different teachers employing different methods, and both employing a different grammatical nomenclature from that used in studying the mother tongue. The classes are encumbered with belated beginners. The child who has got languages from its governess therefore marks time—that is to say, wastes time in these subjects at school. The child well grounded in some foreign tongue is often a source of irritation to the teacher, and gets into trouble because it uses idiomatic expressions with which the teacher is unfamiliar, or seems to reflect upon the teacher's accent. These are the limitations of the school and not the limitations of the pupil. *Given facilities,* there is no reason why there should not be a rapid expansion of the language syllabus at thirteen or fourteen, and why language generally should not be studied. Some Slavonic language could be taken up—Russian or Czech—and a beginning made with some non-Aryan tongue—Arabic, for example.

The object of language teaching in a civilized state is twofold: to give a thorough, intimate, usable knowledge of the mother tongue and of certain key languages. But if teaching were systematic and no time were wasted, if schooling joined on and were continuous instead of being catastrophically disconnected, there is another side of language teaching altogether—now entirely disregarded—and that is the acquisition *in skeleton* of quite a number of languages clustering round the key languages. If at the end of his schooling a boy knows English, French and German very well and nothing more, he is still a helpless foreigner in relation to large parts of the world. But if, in addition, he has an outline knowledge of Russian and Arabic or Turkish or Hindustani—it need only be a quite bare outline—and if he has had a term or so of Spanish in relation to his French, or Swedish in relation to his German, then he has the key in his hands for almost any language he may want. If he has not the language in his head, he has it very conveniently on call—he needs but a sensible conversation dictionary and in a little while he can possess himself of it.

You may think this a large order; you may think I am demanding linguistic prodigies; but remember that I am upon my own ground here; I am a trained teacher and a student of pedagogic science, and I am a watchful parent; I know how time and opportunity are wasted in school, and particularly in language teaching. Languages are not things that exist in isolated subjects; each one illuminates the other and—unless it is taught with stupefying stupidity—leads on to others. A child can acquire the polyglot habit almost unawares. This widening grasp of languages is or was within the capacity of nearly everyone born into the world—given the facilities.

I ask you to note that qualification—"given the facilities."

And now let us turn from the language side to the rest of schooling. A second main division of our schooling was mathematical instruction of a sort. It fell into the three more or less watertight compartments of arithmetic, algebra and Euclid. We carried on in these closed cells what was, I now perceive, a needlessly laborious and needlessly muddled struggle to comprehend quantity, series and form.

In all these matters, looking back upon what I was taught, comparing it with what I now know, and comparing my mind with the minds of more fortunate individuals, I cannot resist the persuasion that I was very badly done indeed in this section. And it is small consolation to me to note that most people's minds seem to be no better done than mine.

My arithmetic, for instance, is mediocre. It is pervaded by inaccuracy. You may say that this is probably want of aptitude. Partly, no doubt, but not altogether. What is want of aptitude? Bad as my arithmetic is now it is not so bad as it was when I left school. When I was about twenty I held a sort of inquest upon it and found out a number of things. I found that I had been allowed to acquire certain bad habits and besetting sins—most people do. For instance, when I ran up a column of figures to add them I would pass from nine to seven quite surely and say sixteen; but if I went from seven to nine I had a vicious disposition to make it eighteen. Endless additions went wrong through that one error. I had fumbled into this vice and—this is my point—my school had no apparatus, and no system of checks, to discover that this had occurred. I used to get my addition wrong and I used to be punished—stupidly—by keeping me in from exercise. Time after time this happened; there was no investigation and no improvement. Nobody ever put me through a series of test sums that would have analyzed my errors and discovered these besetting sins of mine that led to my inaccurate arithmetic.

And another thing that made my arithmetic wrong was a defect in eyesight. My two eyes haven't quite the same focal length and this often puts me out of the straight with a column of figures. But there was nothing in my school to discover that, and my school never did discover it.

My geometrical faculties are also very poor and undeveloped. Euclid's elements, indeed, I have always found simple and straightforward, but when it comes to anything in solid geometry—the intersection of a sphere by a cone, let us say, or something of that sort—I am hopelessly at sea. Deep-seated habits of faulting and fogging, which were actually developed by my schooling, prevent my forming any conception of the surfaces involved.

Here again, just as with the language teaching, hardly any of us are really fully educated. We suffer, nearly all of us, from a lack of quantitative grasp and from an imperfect grasp of form. Few of us have acquired such a grasp. Few of us ever made a proper use of models, and nearly all of us have miserably trained hands. *Given proper facilities*—and here again I ask you to note that proviso—given proper educational facilities— most of us would not only be able to talk with most people in the world but we should also have a conception of form and quantity far more subtle than that possessed by any but a few mathematicians and mechanical geniuses to-day.

Let me now come to a third main division of what we call *schooling*. In our schooling there was an attempt to give us a view of the world about us and a view of our place in it, under the headings of History and Geography.

It would be impossible to imagine a feebler attempt. The History and Geography I had was perhaps, in one respect, the next best thing to a good course. It was so thoroughly and hopelessly bad that it left me with a vivid sense of ignorance.

I read, therefore, with great avidity during my adolescence.

In English schools now I doubt if the teaching of history is much better than it was in my time, but geography has grown and improved—largely through the vigorous initiative of Professor Huxley, who replaced the old dreary topography by a vivid description of the world and mingled with it a sort of *general elementary science* under the name of Physiography. This subject, with the addition of some elementary Biology and Physiology does now serve to give many young people in Great Britain something like a general view of the world as a whole. We need now to make a parallel push with the teaching of history. Upon this matter of the teaching of history I am a fanatic. I cannot think of an education as even half done until there has been a fairly sound review of the whole of the known past, from the beginnings of the geological record up to our own time. Until that is done, the pupil has not been *placed* in the world. He is incapable of understanding his relationship to and his rôle in the scheme of things. He is, whatever else he may have learnt, essentially an ignorant person.

And now let me recapitulate these demands I have made upon the process of schooling—this process of teaching that begins in the nursery and ends about the age of sixteen or seventeen. I have asked that it should involve a practical mastery of three or four languages, including the mother tongue, and that perhaps four or five

other additional languages shall have been
studied, so to speak, in skeleton. I have added
mathematics carried much higher and farther than
most of our schools do to-day. I have demanded
a sound knowledge of universal history, a knowledge of general physical and general biological
science, and I have thrown in, with scarcely a word
of apology, a good training of the eyes and hands
in drawing and manual work.

So far as the pupil goes, I submit this is an
entirely practicable proposal. It can be done, I
am convinced, with any ordinary pupil of average
all-round ability, given—what is now almost universally wanting—the proper educational facilities. And now I will go on to examine the question of why these facilities are wanting. I want
to ask why a large class, if not the whole of our
population, is not educated up to the level of wide
understanding and fully developed capacity such
a schooling as I have sketched out implies.

Well, the first fact obvious to every parent who
has ever enquired closely into the educational outlook of his offspring, the first fact we have to face
is this: there are not enough properly equipped
schools and, still more, not enough good teachers,
to do the job. It is proclaiming no very profound
secret to declare that there is hardly such a thing
in the world to-day as a fully equipped school,
that is to say a school having all the possible material and apparatus and staffed sufficiently with
a bright and able teacher, a really live and alert
educationist, in every necessary subject, such as

would be needed to give this ideal education. That is the great primary obstacle, that is the core of our present problem. We cannot get our modern community educated to anything like its full possibilities as yet because we have neither the teachers nor the schools.

Now is this a final limitation?

For a moment I will leave the question of the possibilities of more and better equipped schools on one side. I will deal with the supply of teachers. At present we do not even attempt to get good teachers; we do not offer any approach to a tolerable life for an ordinary teacher; we compel them to lead mean and restricted lives; we underpay them shockingly; we do not deserve nearly such good teachers as we get. But even supposing we were to offer reasonable wages for teachers; an average all-round wage of £1000 a year or so, and respect and dignity; it does not follow that we should get as many as we should need—using the methods that are in use to-day—to provide this ideal schooling for most of our population, or, indeed, for any large section of our population.

You will note a new proviso creeping in at this point—"using the methods that are used to-day."

Because you must remember it is not simply a matter of payment that makes the teacher. Teachers are born and not made. Good teaching requires a peculiar temperament and distinctive aptitudes. I doubt very much, even if you could secure the services of every human being who had the natural gifts needed in a good teacher, if you could disregard every question of cost and payment, I doubt whether even then you would command the services of more than one passable teacher for a hundred children and of more than one really inspired and inspiring teacher for five hundred children. No doubt you could get *a sort of teacher* for every score or even for every dozen children, a commonplace person who could be trained to do a few simple educational things, but I am speaking now of good teachers who have the mental subtlety, the sympathy and the devotion necessary for efficient teaching by the individualistic methods in use to-day. And since, *using the methods that are used to-day,* you can only hope to secure fully satisfactory results with one teacher to every score of pupils, or fewer, and since it is unlikely we shall ever be able to command the services of more than a tithe of the people who could teach well, it seems that we come up here against an insurmountable obstacle to an educated population.

Now I want to press home the idea of that difficulty. I am an old and seasoned educationist; most of my earliest writings are concealed in the anonymity of the London educational papers of a quarter of a century ago, and my knowledge of educational literature is fairly extensive. I know in particular the literature of educational reform. And I do not recall that I have ever encountered any recognition of this fundamental difficulty in the way of educational development. The literature of educational reform is always assuming parents of limitless intelligence, sympathy and means, employing teachers of limitless energy and capacity. And that to an extreme degree is what we haven't got and what we can never hope to have.

Educational reformers seem always to be looking at education from the point of view of the individual scholastic enterprise and of the individual pupil, and hardly ever from the point of view of a public task dealing with the community as a whole. For all practical purposes this makes waste paper of a considerable proportion of educational literature. This literature, the reader will find, is pervaded by certain fixed ideas. There is a sort of standing objection to any *machining* of education. There is, we are constantly told, to be no syllabus of instruction, no examinations and no controls, no prescribed text-books or diagrams because these things limit the genius of the teacher. And this goes on with a blissful invincible disregard of the fact that in nine hundred and ninety-nine cases out of the thousand the genius of the teacher isn't and can't be there. And also of the fact that this affair of elementary education has in its essentials been done over and over and over again for thousands of millions of times. There ought to be as much scope left for genius and originality in ordinary teaching as there is for genius and originality in a hen laying an ordinary egg.

These educational idealists are always disregarding the fundamental problem of educational

organization altogether, the problem of economy,
economy of the most precious thing of all, *teaching
power*. It is the problem of stretching the competent teacher over the maximum number of
pupils, and that can be done only by the same
methods of economy that are practised in every
other large-scale production—by the standardiza-
tion of everything that can be standardized, and
by the use of every possible time and labour-sav-
ing device and every possible replacement of human effort, not in order to dispense with originality and initiative but in order to conserve them
for application at their points of maximum
efficiency.

I have said that a disregard of the possibilities
of wide organization and its associated economy
of effort is characteristic of most "advanced"
educational literature. You will, if you will examine them, find that disregard working out to its
natural consequences in what are called the "advanced" schools that appeal to educationally anxious parents nowadays. You will find that these
places, often very picturesque and pleasing-look-
ing places, are rarely prosperous enough to maintain more than one or two good teachers. The
rest of the staff shrinks from scrutiny. You will
find these schools adorned with attractive diagrams drawn by the teachers, and strikingly original models and apparatus made by the teachers,
and if you look closely into the matter or consult
an intelligent pupil, you will find there are never
enough diagrams and apparatus to see a course

through. If you press that matter you will find
that they haven't had time to make them so far.
And they will never get so far. No school, however rich and prosperous and however enthusias-
tically run, can hope to make for itself all the
plant and diagrams and apparatus needed for a
fully efficient modern education such as we have
sketched out. As well might a busy man hope
to array himself, by his own efforts, with hats,
suits and boots made by himself out of wool and
raw hides.

But now I think you will begin to see what I
am driving at. It is this: that if the general level
of education is to be raised in our modern community, and if that better education is to be
spread over most of our community, it is necessary
to reorganize education in the world upon entirely
bolder, more efficient, and more economical lines.
We are inexorably limited as to the number of
good teachers we can get into the educational
organization, and we are limited as inexorably as
to the quality of the rank and file of our teaching
profession; but we are not limited in the equipment and systematic organization of teaching
methods and apparatus. That is what I want particularly to enlarge upon now.

Think of the ordinary school-house—a mere
empty brick building with a few hat-pegs, a stale
map or so, half a dozen plaster casts, a few hundred tattered books, a blackboard, and some
broken chemical apparatus: think of it as the
dingy insufficiency it is! In such a place the best

teacher must needs waste three-fourths of his energies. In such a place staff and pupils meet chiefly to waste each other's time. This is the first and principal point at which we can stanch the wastage of teaching energy that now goes on. Everywhere about the world nowadays, the schoolhouse is set up and equipped by a private person or a local authority in more or less complete ignorance of educational possibilities, in more or less complete disconnectedness, without any of the help or any of the economy that comes from a centralized mass production. Let us now consider what we might have in the place of this typical schoolhouse of to-day.

Let me first suggest that every school should have a complete library of very full and explicit lesson notes, properly sorted and classified. All the ordinary subjects in schools have been taught over and over again millions and millions of times. Few people, I think, realize that, and fewer still realize the reasonable consequences of that. Human minds are very much the same everywhere, and the best way of teaching every ordinary school subject, the best possible lesson and the best possible succession of lessons, ought to have been worked out to the last point, and the courses ought to have been stereotyped long ago. Yet if you go into any school to-day, in ninety-nine cases out of the hundred you will find an inexpert and ill-prepared young teacher giving a clumsy, vamped-up lesson as though it had never been given before. He or she will have no proper notes and no proper

diagrams, and a halting and faulty discourse will
be eked out by feeble scratchings with chalk on a
blackboard, by querulous questioning of the
pupils, and irrelevancies. The thing is preposterous.

And linked up with this complete equipment of
proper lesson notes upon which the teacher will
give the lessons, there should be a thing which
does not exist at present in any school and which
ought to exist in every school, a collection of some
hundreds of thousands of pictures and diagrams,
properly and compactly filed; a copious supply of
maps, views of scenery, pictures of towns, and so
forth for teaching geography, diagrams and tables
for scientific subjects, and so on and so on. You
must remember that if the schools of the world
were thought of as a whole and dealt with as a
whole, these things could be produced wholesale at
a cost out of comparison cheaper than they are
made to-day. There is no reason whatever why
school equipment should not be a world market.
A lesson upon the geography of Sweden needs precisely the same maps, the same pictures of scenery,
types of people, animals, cities, and so forth,
whether that lesson is given in China or Peru or
Morocco or London. There is no reason why these
pictures and maps should not be printed from the
same blocks and distributed from the same centre
for the schools of all mankind. If the government
of any large country had the vigour and intelligence to go right ahead and manufacture a proper
equipment of notes and diagrams for its own use

in all its own schools, it would probably be able to recoup itself for most of the outlay by domi-nating the map and diagram markets of the rest of the world.

And next to this full and manageable collection of pictures and diagrams, which the teacher would whip out, with the appropriate notes, five minutes before his lesson began, the modern school would have quite a considerable number of gramophones. These would be used not only to supply music for drill and so forth, and for the analytical study of music, but for the language teaching. Instead of the teacher having to pretend, as he usually pre-tends now, to a complete knowledge of the foreign language he can really only smatter, he would become the honest assistant of the real teaching instrument—the gramophone. Here, again, it is a case for big methods or none—a case for mass production. A mass production of gramophone records for language teaching throughout the world would so reduce the cost that every school could quite easily be equipped with a big repertory of language records. For the first year of any language study, at any rate, the work would go always to the accompaniment of the proper accent and intonation. And all over the world each lan-guage would be taught with the same accent and quantities and idioms—a very desirable thing in-deed.

And now let me pass on to another requirement for an efficient school that our educational organ-ization has still to discover—the method of using the cinematograph. I ask for half a dozen projectors or so in every school, and for a well-stocked store-house of films. The possibilities of certain branches of teaching have been altogether revolutionized by the cinematograph. In nearly every school nowadays you will find a lot of more or less worn and damaged scientific apparatus which is supposed to be used for demonstrating the elementary facts of chemistry, physics and the like. There is a belief that the science teachers—and they do their best with the time and skill and material at their disposal—rig up experimental displays of the more illuminating experimental facts with this damaged litter. Many of us can recall the realities of the sort of demonstration I mean. The performance took two or three hours to prepare, an hour to deliver and an hour or so to clear away; it was difficult to follow, impossible to repeat, it usually went wrong, and almost invariably the teacher lost his temper. These practical demonstrations occurred usually in the opening enthusiasm of the term. As the weeks wore on, the pretence of practical teaching was quietly dropped, and we crammed our science out of the text-book.

Now that is the sort of thing that still goes on. But it ought to be entirely out of date. All that scientific bric-à-brac in the cupboard had far better be thrown away. All the demonstration experiments that science teachers will require in the future can be performed once for all—before a cinematograph. They can be done *finally;* they need never be done again. You can get the best and most dexterous teacher in the world—he can do what has to be done with the best apparatus, in the best light; anything that is very minute or subtle you can magnify or repeat from another point of view; anything that is intricate you can record with extreme slowness; you can show the facts a mile off or six inches off, and all that your actual class teacher need do now is to spend five minutes on getting out the films he wants, ten minutes in reading over the corresponding lecture notes, and then he can run the film, give the lesson, question his class upon it, note what they miss and how they take it, run the film again for a second scrutiny, and get out for the subsequent study of the class the ample supply of diagrams and pictures needed to fix the lesson. Can there be any comparison between the educational efficiency of the two methods?

So I put it to you, that it is possible now to make—and that the world needs badly that we should make—a new sort of school, a standardized school, a school richly equipped with modern apparatus and economizing the labour of teaching to an extent at present undreamt of, in which, all over the world, the same stereotyped lessons, leading the youth of the whole world through a parallel course of schooling, can be delivered.

I know that in putting this before you I challenge some of the most popular affectations of cultivated people. I know that many people will be already writhing with a genteel horror at the idea of the same lesson being given in identical terms to everybody in turn throughout the world. It sounds monotonous. It will rob the world of variety—and so on and so on. But indeed it will not be monotonous at all. That lesson will be new and fresh and good to every pupil who receives it. And remember it is by our hypothesis the best possible form and arrangement of that lesson. It is to take the place of a sham lesson or no lesson at all. There is an eternal freshness in learning as in all the other main things in life. It will be no more monotonous than having one's seventh birthday or falling in love for the first time.

And as for variety, I for one do not care how soon every possible variety of ignorance and misconception is banished from the world. The sun shines on the whole world and it is the same sun. I have still to be persuaded that our planet would be more various and interesting if it were lit by two or three thousand uncertain, spasmodic and differently coloured searchlights directed upon it from every direction. I am pleading for a clear white light of education that shall go like the sun round the whole world.

You see that in all this I am driving at—what shall I call it?—syndicated schools, syndicated lesson notes, and, so far as equipment goes, mass production. I want to see the sort of thing happening to schools that has already happened to many sorts of retail shops. In the place of little ill-equipped schools, each run by its own teacher and buying its own books and diagrams and material and so forth in small quantities at high prices, I want to see a great central organization, employing teachers of genius, working in consultation and co-operation and producing lesson notes, diagrams, films, phonograph records, cheaply, abundantly, on a big scale for a nation, or a group of nations, or, if you like, for all the world, just as America produces watches and alarum clocks and cheap automobiles for all the world. And I want to see the schools of the world being run, so far as the intellectual training goes, not by local committees but by that *central organization*.

It is only by this reorganization of schooling upon the lines of big production that we can hope to get a civilized community in the world at an educational level very markedly higher than the existing educational level.

But if we could so economize teaching energy —if we made our really great teachers, by the use of modern appliances, teachers not of handfuls but of millions; if we insisted upon a universal application of the best and most effective methods of teaching, just as we insist upon the best and most effective methods of street traction and town lighting—then I believe it would be possible to build the civilization of the years to come on a foundation of mental preparation incomparably sounder and higher than anything we know of to-day.

VII

AND now let us go on to the next stages of education.

The schooling process is a natural phase in human development—it is our elaboration of the natural learning of boyhood and girlhood and of adolescence. There was schooling before schools; there was schooling before humanity. I have watched a cat schooling her kittens. Schooling is a part of being young. And we grow up. So there comes a time when schooling is over, when the process of equipment gives place to an increasing share in the activities and decisions of adult life.

Nevertheless for us education must still go on.

I suppose that the savage or the barbarian or the peasant in any part of the world or the uneducated man anywhere would laugh if you told him that the adult must still learn. But in our modern world—I mean the more or less civilized world of the last twenty-five centuries or so—there has grown up a new idea—new, I mean, in the sense that it runs counter to the life scheme of primitive humanity and of most other living things— and that is *the idea that one can go on learning*

167

right up to the end of life. It marks off modern man from all animals, that in his adult life he can display a sense that there remains something still to be investigated and wisdom still to be acquired.

I do not know enough history to tell you with any confidence when adult men, instead of just going about the business of life after they had grown up, continued to devote themselves to learning, to a deliberate prolongation of what is for all other animals an adolescent phase. But by the time of Buddha in India and Confucius in China and the schools of the philosophers in the Greek world the thing was in full progress. That was twenty-six centuries ago or more.

Something of the sort may have been going on in the temples of Egypt or Samaria a score of centuries before. I do not know. You must ask some such great authority as Professor Breasted about that. It may be fifty or a hundred centuries since men, although they were fully grown up, still went on trying to learn.

The idea of adult learning has spread ever since. To-day I suppose most educated people would agree that so long as we live we learn and ought to learn—that we ought to develop our ideas and enlarge, correct and change our ideas.

But even to-day you will find people who have not yet acquired this view. You will find even teachers and doctors and business men who are persuaded that they had learnt all that there was to learn by twenty-five or thirty. It is only quite recently that this idea has passed beyond a special class and pervaded the world generally—the idea of everyone being a life-long student and of the whole world becoming, as it were, a university for those who have passed beyond the schooling stage.

It has spread recently because in recent years the world has changed so rapidly that the idea of settling down for life has passed out of our minds, has given place to a new realization of the need of continuous adaptation to the very end of our days. It is no good settling down in a world that, on its part, refuses to do anything of the sort.

But hitherto, before these new ideas began to spread in our community, the mass of men and women definitely *settled down*. At twelve, or fifteen, or sixteen, or twenty it was decided that they should stop learning. It has only been a rare and exceptional class hitherto that has gone on learning throughout life. The scene and field of that learning hitherto has been in our Western communities the University. Essentially the University is and has been an organization of adult learning as distinguished from preparatory and adolescent learning.

But between the phase of schooling and the phase of adult learning there is an intermediate stage.

In Scotland and America that is distinguished and thought of clearly as the *college stage*. But in England, where we do not think so clearly, this college stage is mixed up with and done partly at school and partly in the University. It is not marked off so definitely from the stage of general preparation that precedes it or from the stage of free intellectual enterprise that follows it.

Now what should college give the young citizen, male or female, upon the foundation of schooling we have already sketched out? In practice we find a good deal of technical study comes into the college stage. The budding lawyer begins to read law, the doctor starts his professional studies, the future engineer becomes technical, and the young merchant sets to work, or should do, to study the great movements of commerce and business method and organization.

As the college stage of those who don't, as a matter of fact, go to college, we have now in every civilized country the evening continuation school, the evening technical school and the works school.

But important as these things are from the point of view of service, they are not the *soul*—not the real meaning of the college stage.

The soul of the college stage, the most important value about it, is that in it is a sort of preparatory pause and inspection of the whole arena of life. It is the educational concomitant of the stage of adolescence.

The young man and the young woman begin to think for themselves, and the college education is essentially the supply of stimulus and material for that process.

It was in the college stage that most of us made out our religion and made it real for ourselves. It was then we really took hold of social and political ideas, when we became alive to literature and art, when we began the delightful and distressful enterprise of finding ourselves.

And I think most of us will agree when we look back that the most real thing in our college life was not the lecturing and the lessons—very much of that stuff could very well have been done in the schooling stage—but the arguments of the debating society, the discussions that broke out in the class-room or laboratory, the talks in one's rooms about God and religion, about the state and freedom, about art, about every possible and impossible social relationship.

Now in addition to that I had something else in my own college course—something of the same sort of thing but better.

I have spoken of myself as undereducated. My schooling was shocking but, as a blessed compensation, my college stage was rather exceptionally good. My schooling ended when I was thirteen. My father, who was a professional cricketer, was smashed up by an accident and I had three horrible years in employment in shops. Then my luck changed and I found myself under one of the very greatest teachers of his time, Professor Huxley. I worked at the Royal College of Science in London for one year under him in his great course in zoology, and for a year and a half under a very good but rather uninspiring teacher, Professor Judd, the geologist. I did also physics and astronomy. Altogether I had three full years of science study. And the teaching of biology at that time, as Huxley had planned it, was a continuing, systematic, illuminating study of life, of the forms and appearances of life, of the way of life, of the interplay of life, of the past of life and the present prospect of life. It was a tremendous training in the sifting of evidence and the examination of appearances.

Every man is likely to be biassed, I suppose, in favour of his own educational course. Yet it seems to me that those three years of work were educational—that they gave a vision of the universe as a whole and a discipline and a power such as no other course, no classical or mathematical course I have ever had a chance of testing, could do.

I am so far a believer in a biological backbone for the college phase of education that I have secured it for my sons and I have done all I can to extend it in England. Nevertheless, important as that formal college work was to me, it still seems to me that the informal part of our college life—the talk, the debates, the discussion, the scampering about London to attend great political meetings, to hear William Morris on Socialism, Auberon Herbert on Individualism, Gladstone on Home Rule, or Bradlaugh on Atheism, for those were the lights of my remote student days—was about equally important.

If schooling is a training in expression and communication, college is essentially the establishment of broad convictions. And in order that they may be established firmly and clearly, it is necessary that the developing young man or woman should hear all possible views and see the medal of truth not only from the obverse but from the reverse side.

Now here again I want to put the same sort of questions I have put about schooling.

Is the college stage of our present educational system anywhere near its maximum possible efficiency? And could it not be extended from its present limited range until it reached practically the whole adolescent community?

Let me deal with the first of these questions first.

Could we not do much more than we do to make the broad issues of various current questions plain and accessible to our students in the college stage?

For example, there is a vast discussion afoot upon the questions that centre upon Property, its rights and its limitations. There is a great literature of Collectivist Socialism and Guild Socialism and Communism. About these things our young people must know. They are very urgent questions; our sons and daughters will have to begin to deal with them from the moment they leave college. Upon them they must form working opinions, and they must know not only what they themselves believe but, if our public affairs are not to degenerate into the squalid, obstinate, hopeless conflicts of prejudiced adherents, they must know also what is believed by other people whose convictions are different from theirs.

You may want to hush these matters up. Many elderly people do. You will fail.

All our intelligent students will insist upon learning what they can of these discussions and forming opinions for themselves. And if the College will not give them the representative books, a fair statement of the facts and views, and some guidance through the maze of these questions, it means merely that they will get a few books in a defiant or underhand way and form one-sided and impassioned opinions.

Another great set of questions upon which the adolescent want to judge for themselves, and ought to judge for themselves, are the religious questions.

And a third group are those that determine the principles of sexual conduct.

I know that in all these matters, on both sides of the Atlantic, a great battle rages between dogma and concealment on the one hand and open ventilation on the other.

Upon the issue I have no doubt. I find it hard even to imagine the case for the former side.

So long as *schooling* goes on, the youngster is immature, needs to be protected, is not called upon for judgments and initiatives, and may well be kept under mental limitations. I do not care very much how you censor or select the reading and talking and thinking of the schoolboy or schoolgirl. But it seems to me that with adolescence comes the right to knowledge and the right of judgment. And that it is the *task and duty* of the college to give matters of opinion in the solid—to let the student walk round and see them from every side.

Now how is this to be done?

I suggest that to begin with we open wide our colleges to propaganda of every sort. There is still a general tendency in universities on both sides of the Atlantic to treat propaganda as infection. For the adolescent it is not—it is a stimulating drug.

Let me instance my own case. I am a man of Protestant origins and with a Protestant habit of mind. But it is a matter of great regret to me that there is no good Roman Catholic propaganda available for my sons in their college life. I would like to have the old Mother Church giving my boys an account of herself and of the part she has played in the history of the world, telling them what she stands for and claims to be, giving her own account of the Mass. These things are interwoven with our past; they are part of us. I do not like them to go into a church and stare like foreigners and strangers at the altar.

And side by side with that Catholic propaganda I would like them to hear an interpretation of religious origins and church history by some non-catholic or sceptical ethnologist. He, too, should be free to tell his story and drive his conclusions home.

But you will find most colleges and most college societies bar religious instruction and discussion. What do they think they are training? Some sort of genteel recluse—or men and women?

So, too, with the discussion of Bolshevism. I do not know how things are in America but in England there has been a ridiculous attempt to suppress Bolshevik propaganda. I have seen a lot of Bolshevik propaganda and it is not very convincing stuff. But by suppressing it, by police seizures of books and papers and the like, it has been invested with a quality of romantic mystery and enormous significance. Our boys and girls, especially the brighter and more imaginative, naturally enough think it must be tremendous stuff to agitate the authorities in this fashion.

At our universities, moreover, the more loutish types of student have been incited to attack and smash up the youths suspected of such reading. This gives it the glamour of high intellectual quality.

The result is that every youngster in the British colleges with a spark of mental enterprise and self-respect is anxious to be convinced of Bolshevik doctrine. He believes in Lenin—because he has been prevented from reading him. Sober collectivists like myself haven't a chance with him.

But you see my conception of the college course? Its backbone should be the study of biology and its substance should be the threshing out of the burning questions of our day.

You may object to this that I am proposing the final rejection of that discipline in classical philosophy which is still claimed as the highest form of college education in the world—the sort of course that the men take in what is called *Greats*

at Oxford. You will accuse me of wanting to bury
and forget Aristotle and Plato, Heraclitus and
Lucretius, and so forth and so on.

But I don't want to do that—*so far as their
thought is still alive.* So far as their thought is
still alive, these men will come into the discussion
of living questions now. If they are Ancients and
dead then let them be buried and left to the ar-
chæological excavator. If they are still Moderns
and alive—I defy you to bury them if you are discussing living questions in a full and honest way.
But don't go hunting after them, there are still
modern Immortals in the darkness of a forgotten
language. Don't make a superstition of them.
Let them come hunting after you. Either they are
unavoidable if your living questions are fully discussed, or they are irrelevant and they do not
matter. That there is a wisdom and beauty in
the classics which is incommunicable in any modern language, which obviously neither ennobles
nor empowers, but which is nevertheless su-
premely precious, is a kind of nonsense dear to the
second-rate classical don, but it has nothing en-
dearing about it for any other human beings. I
will not bother you further with that sort of affec-
tation here.

And this college course I have sketched should,
in the modern state, pass insensibly into adult
mental activities.

Concurrently with it there will be going on, as
I have said, a man's special technical training.
He will be preparing himself for a life of indus-

trialism, commerce, engineering, agriculture, medicine, administration, education or what not. And as with the man, so with the woman. That, too, is a process which in this changing new world of ours can never be completed. Neither of these college activities will ever really leave off. All through his life a man or woman should be confirming, fixing or modifying his or her general opinions; and all the time his or her technical knowledge and power should be consciously increased.

And now let me come to the second problem we opened up in connection with college education—the problem of its extension.

Can we extend it over most or all of a modern population?

I don't think we can, if we are to see it in terms of college buildings, class rooms, tutors, professors and the like. Here again, just as in the case of schooling, we have to raise the neglected problem—neglected so far as education goes—of economy of effort—and we have to look once more at the new facilities that our educational institutions have so far refused to utilize. Our European colleges and universities have a long and honourable tradition that again owes much to the educational methods of the Roman Empire and the Hellenic world. This tradition was already highly developed before the days of printing from movable type, and long before the days when maps or illustrations were printed. The higher education, therefore, was still, as it was in the Stone Age, largely vocal. And the absence of paper and so forth, rendering note-books costly and rare, made a large amount of memorizing necessary. For that reason the mediæval university teacher was always dividing his subject into firstly and secondly and fourthly and sixthly and so on, so that the student could afterwards tick off and reproduce the points on his fingers—a sort of thumb and finger method of thought—still to be found in perfection in the discourses of that eminent Catholic apologist, Mr. Hilaire Belloc. It is a method that destroys all sense of proportion between the headings; main considerations and secondary and tertiary points get all catalogued off as equivalent numbers, but it was a mnemonic necessity of those vanished days.

And they have by no means completely vanished. We still use the lecture as the normal basis of instruction in our colleges, we still hear discourses in the firstly, secondly and thirdly form, and we still prefer even a second-rate professor on the spot to the printed word of the ablest teacher at a distance. Most of us who have been through college courses can recall the distress of hearing a dull and inadequate view of a subject being laboriously unfolded in a long series of tedious lectures, in spite of the existence of full and competent text-books. And here again it would seem that the time has come to centralize our best teaching, to create a new sort of wide teaching professor who will teach not in one college but in many, and to direct the local professor to the more suitable task of ensuring by a commentary, by organized critical work, and so forth, that the text-book is duly read, discussed and compared with the kindred books in the college library.

This means that the great teaching professors will not lecture, or that they will lecture only to try over their treatment of a subject before an intelligent audience as a prelude to publication. They may perhaps visit the colleges under their influence, but their basic instrument of instruction will be not a course of lectures but a book. They will carry out the dictum of Carlyle that the modern university is a university of books.

Now the frank recognition of the book and not the lecture as the substantial basis of instruction opens up a large and interesting range of possibilities. It releases the process of learning from its old servitude to place and to time. It is no longer necessary for the student to go to a particular room, at a particular hour, to hear the golden words drop from the lips of a particular teacher. The young man who reads at eleven o'clock in the morning in luxurious rooms in Trinity College, Cambridge, will have no very marked advantage over another young man, employed during the day, who reads at eleven o'clock at night in a bed-sitting-room in Glasgow. The former, you will say, may get commentary and discussion, but there is no particular reason why the latter should not form some sort of reading society with his fellows, and discuss the question with them in the dinner hour and on the way to the works. Nor is there any reason why he should not get tutorial help as a university extension from the general educational organization, as good in quality as any other tutorial help.

And this release of the essentials of a college education from limitations of locality and time brought about by modern conditions, not only makes it unnecessary for a man to come "up" to college to be educated, but abolishes the idea that his educational effort comes to an end when he goes "down." Attendance at college no longer justifies a claim to education; inability to enter a college is no longer an excuse for illiteracy.

I do not think that our educational and university authorities realize how far the college stage of education has already escaped from the local limitations of colleges; they do not understand what a great and growing volume of adolescent learning and thought, of college education in the highest and best sense of the word, goes on outside the walls of colleges altogether; and on the other they do not grasp the significant fact that, thanks to the high organization of sports and amusements and social life in our more prosperous universities, a great proportion of the youngsters who come in to their colleges never get the realities of a college education at all, and go out into the world again as shallow and uneducated as they came in. And this failure to grasp the great change in educational conditions brought about, for the most part, in the last half century, accounts for the fact that when we think of any extension of

higher education in the modern community we are
all too apt to think of it as a great proliferation of
expensive, pretentious college buildings and a
great multiplication of little teaching professor-
ships, and a further segregation of so many hundreds or thousands of our adolescents from the
general community, when as a matter of fact the
reality of education has ceased to lie in that direction at all.   The modern task is not to multiply
teachers *but to exalt and intensify exceptionally
good teachers,* to recognize their close relationship with the work of university research—which
it is their business to digest and interpret—and to
secure the production and wide distribution of
books throughout the community.

I am inclined to think that the type of adolescent education, very much segregated in out-of-
the-way colleges and aristocratic in spirit, such
as goes on now at Oxford, Cambridge, Yale, Hol-
loway, Wellesley and the like, has probably
reached and passed its maximum development.   I
doubt if the modern community can afford to continue it; it certainly cannot afford to extend it very
widely.

But as I have pointed out, there has always
been a second strand to college education—the
technical side, the professional training or appren-
ticeship.   Here there are sound reasons that the
student should go to a particular place, to the
special museums and laboratories, to the institutes
of research, to the hospitals, factories, works,
ports, industrial centres and the like where the

realities he studies are to be found, or to the studios or workshops or theatres where they practise the art to which he aspires. Here it seems we have natural centres of aggregation in relation to which the college stage of a civilized community, the general adolescent education, the vision of the world as a whole and the realization of the individual place in it, can be organized most conveniently.

You see that what I am suggesting here is in effect that we should take our colleges, so far as they are segregations of young people for general adolescent education, and break them as a cook breaks eggs—and stir them up again into the general intellectual life of the community.

Coupled with that there should, of course, be a proposal to restrict the hours of industrial work or specialized technical study up to the age of twenty, at least, in order to leave time for this college stage in the general education of every citizen of the world.

The idea has already been broached that men and women in the modern community are no longer inclined to consider themselves as ever completely adult and finished; there is a growing disposition and a growing necessity to keep on learning throughout life. In the worlds of research, of literature and art and economic enterprise, that adult learning takes highly specialized forms which I will not discuss now; but in the general modern community the process of continuing education after the college stage is still evidently

only at a primitive level of development. There
are a certain number of literary societies and societies for the study of particular subjects; the pul-
pit still performs an educational function; there
are public lectures and in America there are the
hopeful germs of what may become later on a very
considerable organization of adult study in the
Lyceum Chautauqua system; but for the generality of people the daily newspaper, the Sunday
newspaper, the magazine and the book constitute
the only methods of mental revision and enlargement after the school or college stage is past.

Now we have to remember that the bulk of this
great organization of newspapers and periodicals
and all the wide distribution of books that goes on
to-day are extremely recent things. This new
nexus of print has grown up in the lifetime of four
or five generations, and it is undergoing constant
changes. We are apt to forget its extreme new-
ness in history and to disregard the profound difference in mental conditions it makes between our
own times and any former period. It is impossible
to believe that thus far it is anything but a sketch
and intimation of what it will presently be. It
has grown. No man foresaw it; no one planned
it. We of this generation have grown up with
it and are in the habit of behaving as though this
nexus had always been with us and as though it
would certainly remain with us. The latter
conclusion is almost wilder than the former.

By what we can only consider a series of fortunate accidents, the press and the book world

have provided and do provide a necessary organ in the modern world state, an organ for swift general information upon matters of fact and for the rapid promulgation and diffusion of ideas and interpretations. The newspaper grew, as we know, out of the news letter which in a manuscript form existed before the Roman Empire; it owes its later developments largely to the advertisement possibilities that came with the expansion of the range of trading as the railways and suchlike means of communication developed. Modern newspapers have been described, not altogether inaptly, as sheets of advertisements with news and discussions printed on the back. The extension of book reading from a small class, chiefly of men, to the whole community has also been largely a response to new facilities; though it owes something also to the religious disputes of the last three centuries. The population of Europe, one may say with a certain truth, first learnt to read the Bible, and only afterwards to read books in general. A large proportion of the book publishing in the English language in the seventeenth and eighteenth centuries still consisted of sermons and controversial theological works.

Both newspaper and book production began in a small way as the enterprise of free individuals, without anyone realizing the dimensions to which the thing would grow. Our modern press and book trade, in spite of many efforts to centralize and control it, in spite of Defence of the Realm Acts and the like, is still the production of an unorganized multitude of persons. It is not centralized; it is not controlled. To this fact the nexus of print owes what is still its most valuable quality. Thoughts and ideas of the most varied and conflicting sort arise and are developed and worked out and fought out in this nexus, just as they do in a freely thinking vigorous mind.

I am not, you will note, saying that this freedom is perfect or that the thought process of the print nexus could not go very much better than it does, but I am saying that it has a very considerable freedom and vigour and that so far as it has these qualities it is a very fine thing indeed.

Now many people think that we are moving in the direction of world socialism to-day. Collectivism is perhaps a better, more definite word than socialism, and, so far as keeping the peace goes, and in matters of transport and communication, trade, currency, elementary education, the production and distribution of staples and the conservation of the natural resources of the world go, I believe that the world and the common sense of mankind move steadily towards a world collectivism. But the more co-operation we have in our common interests, the more necessary is it to guard very jealously the freedom of the mind, that is to say, the liberty of discussion and suggestion.

It is here that the Communist régime in Russia has encountered its most fatal difficulty. A catastrophic unqualified abolition of private property has necessarily resulted in all the paper, all the printing machinery, all the libraries, all the news-stalls and book shops, becoming Government property. It is impossible to print anything without the consent of the Government. One cannot buy a book or newspaper; one must take what the Government distributes. Free discussion—never a very free thing in Russia—has now on any general scale become quite impossible. It was a difficulty foreseen long ago in Socialist discussions, but never completely met by the thorough paced Communist. At one blow the active mental life of Russia has been ended, and so long as Russia remains completely and consistently communist it cannot be resumed. It can only be resumed by some surrender of paper, printing and book distribution from absolute Government ownership to free individual control. That can only be done by an abandonment of the full rigours of communist theory.

In our western communities the dangers to the intellectual nexus lie rather on the other side. The war period produced considerable efforts at Government control and as a consequence considerable annoyance to writers, much concealment and some interference with the expression of opinion; but on the whole both newspapers and books held their own. There is to-day probably as much freedom of publishing as ever there was. It is not from the western governments that mischief is likely to come to free intellectual activity in the western communities but from the undisciplined individual, and from the incitements to mob violence by various propagandist religions and cults against free discussion.

About the American press I know and can say little. I will speak only of things with which I am familiar. I am inclined to think that there has been a considerable increase of deliberate lying in the British press since 1914, and a marked loss of journalistic self-respect. Particular interests have secured control of large groups of papers and pushed their particular schemes in entire disregard of the general mental well-being. For instance, there has recently been a remarkable boycott in the London press of a very able collectivist book, Sir Leo Money's "Triumph of Nationalization" because it would have interfered with the operation of very large groups which were concerned in getting back public property into private hands on terms advantageous to the latter. It is a book not only important as a statement of a peculiar economic view, but because of the statesmanlike gravity and clearness of its exposition. I do not think it would have been possible to stand between the public and a writer in this way in the years before 1914. A considerable proportion of the industrial and commercial news is now written to an end. The British press has also suffered greatly from the outbreak of social and nationalist rancour arising out of the great war, the inability of the European mind to grasp the Bolshevik issue, and the clumsy blunderings of the Versailles settlement. Quite half the news from Eastern Europe that appears in the London press is now

deliberate fabrication, and a considerable proportion of the rest is rephrased and mutilated to give
a misleading impression to the reader.

But people cannot be continuously deceived in
this way, and the consequence of this press de-
moralization has been a great loss of influence for
the daily paper. A diminishing number of people
now believe the news as it is given them, and fewer
still take the unsigned portions of the newspaper
as written in good faith. And there has been a
consequent enhancement of the importance of
signed journalism. Men of manifest honesty, men
with names to keep clean, have built up reputa-
tions and influence upon the ruins of editorial
prestige. The exploitation of newspapers by the
adventurers of "private enterprise" in business,
has carried with it this immense depreciation in
the power and honour of the newspaper.

I am inclined to think that this swamping of a
large part of the world's press by calculated falsehood and partizan propaganda is a temporary
phase in the development of the print nexus:
nevertheless, it is a very great inconvenience and
danger to the world. It stands very much in the
way of that universal adult education which is our
present concern. Reality is horribly distorted.
Men cannot see the world clearly and they cannot,
therefore, begin to think about it rightly.

We need a much better and more trustworthy
press than we possess. We cannot get on to a
new and better world without it. The remedy is
to be found not, I believe, in any sort of Govern-

ment control, but in a legal campaign against the one thing harmful—the lie. It would be in the interests of most big advertisers—for most big advertisement is honest; it would be, in the long run, in the interests of the press, and it would mean an enormous step forward in the general mental clarity of the world if a deliberate lie, whether in an advertisement or in the news or other columns of the press, was punishable—punishable whether it did or did not involve anything that is now an actionable damage. And it would still further strengthen the print nexus and clear the mind of the world if it were compulsory to correct untrue statements in the periodical press, whether they had been made in good faith or not, at least as conspicuously and lengthily as the original statement. I can see no impossibility in the realization of either of these proposals, and no objection that a really honest newspaper proprietor or advertiser could offer to them. It would make everyone careful, of course, but I fail to see any grievance in that. The sanitary effect upon the festering disputes of our time would be incalculably great. It would be like opening the windows upon a stuffy, overcrowded and unventilated room of disputing people.

Given adequate laws to prevent the cornering of paper or the partizan control of the means of distribution of books and printed matter, I believe that the present freedoms and the unhampered individualism of the world of thought, discussion and literary expression are and must remain conditions essential to the proper growth and activity of a common world mind. On the basis of that sounder education I have sketched in a preceding paper, there is possible such an extension of understanding, such an increase of intelligent co-operations and such a clarification of wills as to dissolve away half the difficulties and conflicts of the present time and to provide for the other half such a power of solution as we, in the heats, entanglements and limitations of our present ignorance, doubt and misinformation can scarcely begin to imagine.

I do not know how far I have conveyed to you in the last two papers my underlying idea of an education not merely intensive but extensive, planned so economically and so ably as to reach every man and woman in the world.

It is a dream not of *individuals educated*—we have thought too much of the individual educated *for* the individual—but of a *world educated* to a pitch of understanding and co-operation far beyond anything we know of to-day, for the sake of all mankind.

I have tried to show that, given organization, given the will for it, such a world-wide education is possible.

I wish I had the gift of eloquence so that I could touch your wills in this matter. I do not know how this world of to-day strikes upon you. I am not ungrateful for the gift of life. While there is life and a human mind, it seems to me there must always be excitements and beauty, even if the excitements are fierce and the beauty terrible and tragic. Nevertheless, this world of mankind to-day seems to me to be a very sinister and dreadful world. It has come to this—that I open my newspaper every morning with a sinking heart, and usually I find little to console me. Every day there is a new tale of silly bloodshed. Every day I read of anger and hate, oppression and misery and want—stupid anger and oppression, needless misery and want—the insults and suspicions of ignorant men, and the inane and horrible self-satisfaction of the well-to-do. It is a vile world because it is an undereducated world, unreasonable, suspicious, base and ferocious. The air of our lives is a close and wrathful air; it has the closeness of a prison—the indescribable offence of crowded and restricted humanity.

And yet I know that there is a way out.

Up certain steps there is a door to this dark prison of ignorance, prejudice and passion in which we live—and that door is only locked on the inside. It is within our power, given the will for it, given the courage for it—it is within our power to go out. The key to all our human disorder is organized education, comprehensive and universal. The watchword of conduct that will clear up all our difficulties is the *plain truth*. Rely upon that watchword, use that key with courage and we can go out of the prison in which we live; we can go right out of the conditions of war, shortage, angry scrambling, mutual thwarting and malaise and disease in which we live; we and our kind can go out into sunlight, into a sweet air of understanding, into confident freedoms and a full creative life—for ever.

I do not know—I do not dare to believe—that I shall live to hear that key grating in the lock. It may be our children and our children's children will still be living in this jail. But a day will surely come when that door will open wide and all our race will pass out from this magic prison of ignorance, suspicion and indiscipline in which we now all suffer together.

VIII

THE ENVOY

In the preceding papers I have, with some repetition and much stumbling, set out a fairly complete theory of what men and women have to do at the present time if human life is to go on hopefully to any great happiness and achievement in the days to come. Much of this material was first prepared to be delivered to a lecture audience, and I regret that ill-health has prevented a complete re-writing of these portions. There is more of the uplifted forefinger and the reiterated point than I should have allowed myself in an essay. But this is a loss of grace rather than of clearness. And since I am stating a case and not offering the reader anything professing to be a literary work, I shall not apologize for finally summing up and underlining the chief points of this book.

They are, firstly: that a great change in human conditions has been brought about during the past century, and secondly that a vast task of adaptation, which must be, initially and fundamentally, *mental* adaptation, has to be undertaken by our race. It is a task which politicians, who live from day to day, and statesmen, who live from event to event, may hinder or aid very greatly, but which they cannot be expected to conduct or control. Politicians and statesmen perforce live and work in the scheme of ideas they find about them; the conditions of their activities are made for them. They can be compelled by the weight of public opinion to help it, but the driving force for this great task must come not from official sources but from the steadfast educational pressure of a great and growing multitude of convinced people. In times of fluctuation and dissolving landmarks, the importance of the teacher—using the word in its widest sense—rises with the progressive dissolution of the established order.

The creative responsibility for the world to-day passes steadily into the hands of writers and school teachers, students of social and economic science, professors and poets, editors and journalists, publishers and newspaper proprietors, preachers, every sort of propagandist and every sort of disinterested person who can give time and energy to the reconstruction of the social idea. Human life will continue to be more and more dangerously chaotic until a world social idea crystallizes out. That—and no existing institution and no current issue—is the primary concern of the present age.

We need, therefore, before all other sorts of organization, educational organizations; we need, before any other sort of work, work of education and enlightenment; we need everywhere active societies pressing for a better, more efficient conduct of public schooling, for a wider, more enlight-

ening school curriculum, for a world-wide linking
up of educational systems, for a ruthless subordination of naval, military and court expenditure
to educational needs, and for a systematic dis-
couragement of mischief-making between nation
and nation and race and race and class and class.
I could wish to see Educational Societies, organized as such, springing up everywhere, watching
local bodies in order to divert economies from the
educational starvation of a district to other less
harmful saving; watching for obscurantism and
reaction and mischievous nationalist teaching in
the local schools and colleges and in the local
press; watching members of parliament and con-
gressmen for evidences of educational good-will
or malignity; watching and getting control of the
administration of public libraries; assisting, when
necessary, in the supply of sound literature in
their districts; raising funds for invigorating educational propaganda in poor countries like China
and in atrociously educated countries like Ireland,
and corresponding with kindred societies throughout the world.   I believe such societies would
speedily become much more influential than the
ordinary political party clubs and associations
that now use up so much human energy in the
western communities.   Subordinating all vulgar
political considerations to educational development as the supreme need in the world's affairs,
even quite small societies could exercise a powerful decisive voice in a great number of political
contests.   And an educational movement is more

tenacious than any other sort of social or political
movement whatever. It trains its adherents.
What it wins it holds.

I know that in thus putting all the importance
upon educational needs at the present time I shall
seem to many readers to be ignoring quite ex-
cessively the profound racial, social and economic
conflicts that are in progress. I do. I believe we
shall never get on with human affairs until we do
ignore them. I offer no suggestion whatever as to
what sides people should take in such an issue as
that between France and Germany or between
Sinn Fein and the British Government, or in the
class war. I offer no such suggestion because I
believe that all these conflicts and all such current
conflicts are so irrational and destructive that it
is impossible for a sane man who wishes to serve
the world to identify himself with either side in
any of them. These conflicts are mere aspects of
the gross and passionate stupidity and ignorance
and sectionalism of our present world. The class
war, the push for and the resistance to some vague
reorganization called the Social Revolution—such
things are the natural inevitable result of the sor-
did moral and intellectual muddle of our common
ideas about property. The capitalist, the employer, the property-owning class, as a class, have
neither the intelligence nor the conscience to comprehend any moral limitations, any limitations
whatever but the strong arm of the law, upon what
they do with their property. Their black and obstinate ignorance, the clumsy adventurousness

they call private enterprise, their unconscious in-
solence to poor people, their stupidly conspicuous
self-indulgence, produce as a necessary result the
black hatred of the employed and the expropri-
ated. On one side we have greed, insensibility and
incapacity, on the other envy and suffering stung
to vindictive revolt; on neither side light nor gen-
erosity nor creative will. Neither side has any
power to give us any reality we need. Neither
side is more than a hate and an aggression. How
can one take sides between them?

The present system, *unless it can develop a better intelligence and a better heart,* is manifestly
destined to foster fresh wars and to continue wast-
ing what is left of the substance of mankind, until
absolute social disaster overtakes us all. And
manifestly the revolutionary communist, *at his
present level of education,* has neither the plans
nor the capacity to substitute any more efficient
system for this crazy edifice of ill-disciplined private enterprise that is now blundering to destruction. But at a higher level of intelligence, at a
level at which it is possible to define the limitations
of private property clearly and to ensure a really
loyal and effectual co-operation between individual
and state, this issue—this wholly destructive conflict between the property manipulator and the
communist fanatic which is now rapidly wreck-
ing our world—disappears. It disappears as
completely as the causes of a murderous conflict
between two drunken men will disappear when

they are separated and put under a stream of clear cold water.

So it is that, in spite of their apparent urgency, I ask the reader to detach himself from these present conflicts of national politics, of political parties and of the class war as completely as he can; or, if he cannot detach himself completely, then to play such a part in them, regardless of any other consideration, as may be most conducive to a wide-thinking, wide-ranging education upon which we can base a new world order. A resolute push for quite a short period now might reconstruct the entire basis of our collective human life.

In this book I have tried to show what form that push should take, to show that it has a reasonable hope of an ultimate success, and that unless it is made, the outlook for mankind is likely to become an entirely dismal prospect. I put these theses before the reader for his consideration. They are not discursive criticisms of life, not haphazard grumblings at our present discontents, they are offered as the fundamental propositions of an ordered constructive project in which he can easily find a part to play commensurate with his ability and opportunities.

13566